D0862363

PERMISSION TO TRY

11 Things You Need to Hear
WHEN YOU'RE SCARED
TO CHANGE YOUR LIFE

ANNIE FRANCESCHI

Greatest
Story
Publishing

DURHAM,
NORTH CAROLINA

The events and conversations in this book have been set down to the best of the author's ability, with great respect for those referenced. Some names and details have been changed to protect the privacy of individuals who are, perhaps, not ready to be super-famous by way of this book.

The advice provided is meant to be seasoned with however many grains of salt you feel appropriate to make the best decisions in your own life and career. Remember you're in the driver's seat of what you do before, during, and after picking up these pages. When you think about it, that's a pretty great thing.

While the author plans to provide online access to this book's bonus resources (templates, etc.) for some time, she makes no claim that these resources will always be available to the reader. This is for various reasons including the nature of the internet and the possibility that we may all live on Mars where someday such resources may become too expensive to host. The author is also not responsible for availability or any other aspect of external referenced content such as video links, other book titles, etc.

Published in Durham, North Carolina by Greatest Story Publishing, an imprint of Greatest Story Creative™. Greatest Story Creative is a federally registered trademark of Greatest Story Creative LLC.

This book may be purchased in bulk at special pricing for educational, business, or personal use and the author is available for speaking, events, and interviews. To purchase multiple copies or to connect with the author for press, speaking engagements and more, contact us at info@greateststorycreative.com.

First paperback edition October 2018.

Cover and book design by Annie Franceschi
Edited by Jodi Brandon
Photography (unless otherwise noted) by Faith Teasley Photography, faithteasley.com

ISBN 978-1-7326859-0-1

Library of Congress Control Number: 2018957294
Printed in the United States of America

Contents

PERMISSION
PART ONE

———

Rethink Your Purpose

PERMISSION
PART TWO

———

Embrace Change and Take Action

For my dad, Michael, who a
cares about what I have to say.

And for my husband, Gus,
who is always the first to tell me,
"You can do it."

PERMISSION

PART THREE

———

Face Your Feelings, Failures, and Fears

JUST FOR YOU

———

Discovering Permission

Thinking about changing your life? Wondering about switching careers? Feeling stuck? Maybe it'd be good to sit down to coffee with someone who's been there. If you and I got together today, here are some things I'd share with you.

Years ago, I also wanted to change my life but I had a million reasons why I was too scared to. At the time, I was working at Disney. Not the theme parks—the filmmaking studios in Burbank, California. It was a "wildest dreams" opportunity. I'd grown up obsessed with storytelling: from loving movies, to writing screenplays in high school and doing film internships around the world in college.

It was still hard to believe that every day I was working on the very same lot that Walt Disney bought with the proceeds of *Snow White and the Seven Dwarves.* I was a founding member of "Franchise Management," an exciting team that did communications and product development for upcoming films. Part of my role was to create, write, and design story presentations about big-time movies like *Maleficent*, the live action *Cinderella*, and others.

But while I had this big, sexy job and was walking the path to Hollywood success, I was also feeling lost, stuck, and confused about what to do next. I knew then, though I was afraid to admit it to myself, that my impressive career just didn't feel right. My dream wasn't turning out how I thought it would.

The worries that crossed my mind daily were things like—

- *Why am I not happy with my life if I'm "living my dream"?*
- *Does that mean this path isn't my dream, after all?*
- *Oy, but I told everyone "this" was my dream! Crap. This is embarrassing.*
- *What would it mean to admit I made a mistake? . . . Is it a mistake?*
- *If I'm not meant to do this, what the heck else am I supposed to do?*
- *Maybe I could try something on the side . . .*
- *But what if I get in trouble?*

I had lots of questions and not a ton of answers.

It was the summer of 2012. I was in an Urban Outfitters in Burbank, waiting to meet friends for a movie. To kill time, I picked up a book that caught my eye: *Steal Like an Artist: 10 Things Nobody Ever Told You About Being Creative* by Austin Kleon.

I breezed through most of this little 6x6" book in about 30 minutes, standing right there in the store. In this engaging read, Austin shares his favorite principles for being more creative in how you approach your work and life. His second chapter, "Don't Wait Until You Know Who You Are to Get Started," hit me like a ton of bricks. That's exactly what I'd been doing: waiting. Reading these words gave me something I never expected: permission I had *no idea* I was looking for. It was permission to answer all those questions in my head— permission to embark into the unknown.

I had been wanting to try some new things and get my feet wet outside "the one path" I'd told everyone that I was on. The book woke me up and told me that it's okay to do whatever it is that's on your heart to do. The advice gave me permission to try, despite my fears and uncertainty. It showed me a way to create my own new path by putting one foot in front of the other and then growing from whatever happened next.

Later that same year, fueled by Austin Kleon's little book of creative advice, I started a blog called anniemade to promote a small wedding side business I had launched that fall. In the winter, the blog and a Google inquiry from a bride turned into a freelance graphic design and writing business. Shortly after that, I had the confidence and inkling enough of a purpose to quit my "dream job" at Disney and move from California back home to North Carolina. And that purpose ultimately became starting my own branding agency, Greatest Story Creative, one year later in the fall of 2013.

I had no way to know the dominos would fall like they did just by starting that little online shop and blog, but I've kept pushing them over to more great things.

In the five years that have followed from founding Greatest Story, I've become a locally known brand creator and a professional speaker here in North Carolina. I've advised and taught branding to hundreds of business owners. I've told the stories of more than 70 businesses through creating their written and visual branding (names, logos, taglines, websites, etc.). I've spoken to thousands of people on branding, entrepreneurship, and rewriting your dreams. While it's never been an easy or straightforward path, this has turned out to be a kind of success that finally feels right to me. I truly love what I do and I'm incredibly grateful for the life I have, even though I never once would have imagined that *this* is where my career would go.

Quite often, I think of the spark that started it all—the spark I needed that I got from a short, little book you can read in one sitting. In a lot of ways, it lit the fuse of everything that's followed and led me here. Looking back has had me wondering: What would I tell "Past Annie" from years ago? What would I say to her when she was feeling lost about what to do next? And what might I tell you if we actually did sit down for coffee and you said, *"I'm thinking of changing my life, but how do I do it? And should I do it?"*

It all comes down to permission: how we are the last to give it to ourselves, and how we tend to look to everyone and everything else for it. Looking for permission keeps us stuck in jobs we hate, relationships that are toxic, and lives we don't enjoy living. When it comes to seeking permission from others or the universe, we do this even (and maybe especially) when it comes to the greatest choices of our lives.

The reality of my own success story is that I'd had it in me all along to reinvent my life and my career. From the blog to my business today, the nuggets of every one of the milestones I've reached with my new dreams had been hanging out in the back of my brain for years before I ever gave myself permission for them to be possible.

They almost never happened at all, and that's because I was afraid.

I let the fear of change rule me for too many years. It took standing in the book section at Urban Outfitters and an author and artist named Austin Kleon to give me the permission I needed when I just couldn't give it to myself. And that's what I want this book to be for you.

You need to know that we all worry that we're not on the right path. At any age, we don't know what we want to be when we grow up. And we want to make change happen, but quite often, we are afraid to give ourselves permission to try.

So it's time to cut out the middle man.

You've got real worries:

> *What will other people say?*
> *What if I fail?*
> *What would I do instead?*

And you deserve to know what's on the other side of those fears. I'm going to show you what the other side looks like and lead you to the permission to do the things that scare you—the same things that you can't get out of your brain.

This book is here to be the permission to reinvent yourself and the courage to keep going into the unknown, even when you don't know who you are just yet. I'm going to tell you what I'd wish I'd known then, what I've learned along the way, and what I want to remember when I find myself at a crossroads again.

Turn the page. What follows is what you need to hear.

How This Book Was Built for You

This book is for you if you're:

- Considering changing careers.
- Contemplating a big life change or move.
- Feeling lost in-between jobs.
- Thinking of starting a business.
- Looking for the confidence to do something new.
- Stuck and afraid of change.
- Wondering about taking a big risk.

And this book is here to speak directly to the arguments running through your head right now about where you are.

When we're considering taking a big risk in our lives, we are quick to stop and argue with ourselves. We imagine a great step we could take to move forward. But then what happens? We immediately think of a compelling reason why we're afraid to and shouldn't do it.

So that's exactly how this book is organized. You've got solid concerns about doing something big, exciting, and scary. In turn, I've got 11 things you need to hear about them before you stop yourself from starting.

Built as a three-part plan designed to help you summon your courage, this text contains new perspectives and encouragement in the form of hard-won personal stories, funny anecdotes, and even "take action" exercises, all drawn from what I went through to get a life that I love. One by one, these pages are here to knock down the objections and replace them with something much more powerful: *possibility*.

As you read, keep in mind the big things you've been thinking about doing. Let this be your pep talk to make what matters to you happen. And though you're starting where we all do (facing your current reality), hopefully you'll soon close the last page of this book having taken several valuable steps on the way to changing your life.

Ready? Let's get going.

PERMISSION
PART ONE

————

Rethink
Your Purpose

CHAPTER 1

DOUBT:

*"But this path was supposed to
make me happy."*

PERMISSION:

IT'S OKAY TO REWRITE YOUR DREAM

You Don't Have to Know
What You Want to Be

When I was in the film industry, I'd set up coffee and lunch meetings often to network. They were with people at all different levels of a company, from assistants to senior vice presidents—basically, anyone who would say *yes*. I wanted to learn all that I could, from as many people as I could. In doing this, I discovered that everyone had something to teach me.

One of these coffees was with Jay Aquilanti. At the time, Jay had what I'd absolutely call a dream job. He was the director of franchise at Walt Disney Imagineering (you know, the theme park people!). We met at the Imagineering campus in Glendale and enjoyed a commissary lunch in California sunshine.

At the time, I was a coordinator and trying to figure out how I was going to climb the ladder and get to that real "dream work" that I was thinking I was meant to do. I remember looking up to him, imagining he was totally set and had "made it" career-wise. He was living the dream I wanted someday. So I felt pretty wise picking Jay's brain about my current role. I asked him what I should do next. How could I get to his level of career nirvana?

Jay is a jovial and bold guy. He's the kind of person who picks up on it if you're being shy and won't let you hide. If he spots you avoiding eye contact, he's the type to loudly say, "Hello, good morning. How's your day going?" And of course when that happens, you can't help but smile and match his energy. But on that particular day, when I asked for Jay's advice, his tone got a bit more serious and intentional.

He looked at me thoughtfully and said, "Annie, I'm 42 and I still don't know what I want to be when I grow up."

I still don't know what I want to be when I grow up.

At the time, his words were surprising. Here was Jay, rocking an amazing job for one of the greatest companies on the planet, yet he still doesn't know what he wants to be when he grows up or what his one "final purpose" is. Even now as a catalyst director at Disney's Yellow Shoes Creative Group, he's still dreaming, thinking, doing—figuring it out. To this day, I think about how freeing his answer was.

I still don't know what I want to be when I grow up.

Not knowing what you want to be when you grow up—I've felt that way. And I still sometimes do, even as much as I love the work I'm doing. Do you ever feel that way? YES !!!

This isn't something we leave behind when we're 6 or 60. We're not alone in this. We're all in the process of remaking and reinventing ourselves in some way. The purpose that brought us to our first career may not be the same purpose we identify with now. You're not the person you were a year ago or five years ago. You won't be the same person a few years from now . . . so why all this pressure to have it all wrapped up today?

Media mogul Martha Stewart, car inventor Henry Ford, dress designer Vera Wang, author Laura Ingalls Wilder, and actor Samuel L. Jackson have something in common: They didn't find their "thing" and hit it big until they were in their 40s. Martha Stewart didn't even have her signature TV show until age 51. Vera Wang decided to start designing wedding dresses when she got married at age 40. Laura Ingalls Wilder didn't publish her famous *Little House* book series until she was 65.

If, after many decades, these impressive folks still had time to figure out what they wanted to be when they grew up, guess what? So do you.

It's All Right if Your Dream Hasn't Turned Out as Planned

For years, I think I knew deep-down, in the very back of my head, that the film industry wasn't for me. But that realization scared the crap out of me. For the longest time, I couldn't face that truth. I couldn't admit it to myself because I was worried about all the things that would mean.

It would mean that I was admitting failure.
It would mean people would judge me.
It would mean total uncertainty ahead.
It would force me to ask myself: If I'm not this—then who *am* I?

I didn't have good answers and I didn't have a way out—yet.

And in that time, I felt so much disappointment and discontent. But with that in my heart, I had to keep climbing the corporate ladder— staying the course on what I told everyone my dream was (or I was risking doom and eternal professional abyss). In those moments, and so much sooner than I'd realized it, I wish I'd known it was okay to change course in my career and in my life.

It's okay that your dream doesn't work out the way you planned or the *way you told everyone it was going to.*

If you know in the back of your mind that things aren't right, know that it's normal for this to happen. It's not something you have to be paralyzed in fear about; fear just keeps you going d⸏⸏⸏⸏ ⸏⸏⸏ng road.

Talk about going down the wrong road. I spent so

up and down the 405, from Sherman Oaks to Santa Monica, or from Culver City to Burbank, in tears wondering, *Why is my "dream" not working out?*

I'd wanted to be in the film industry since I was a teenager. I had always been the "arts" kid. (I'm definitely not the "sports" kid. I always got hit in the head with the ball—even whiffle ball.) I was always winning writing competitions, thriving in art class, and recruiting the entire high school of Fayetteville Academy to perform Disney musicals with me. And I grew up going to the movies with my dad. We've probably seen at least 1,000 movies together (I counted once). One night in high school, I got an idea to write a feature-length screenplay. I wrote one in a week with the help of *The Screenwriter's Bible*, and my original dream was born:

Write and work on movies that tell great stories.

From then on, I planned to follow "the one path" to make it in the movie industry. I went on to write three more scripts during high school and one more at Duke University. While at Duke, I did some summer internships at different film companies (in DC, London, and LA) and created a 24-hour film competition: the Movie Making Marathon. And then I did what anyone who lives in North Carolina has to do if they have dreams of working in the movie business: I moved.

I moved 3,000 miles across the country to Los Angeles, California, and I was ready! I'd written five screenplays, produced two years of film-related events, and done three film studio internships. *Let me write a movie.* I snagged my first gig: an executive intern to the president of Lionsgate Films. My job was acting as the second assistant (an assistant to the first assistant—*seriously*). I learned pretty quickly that I wouldn't be writing movies as much as I'd be writing expense reports. But the film industry is an apprentice sort of industry, so I hung in there.

Once I was working in LA, I started to realize this path I'd started down wasn't quite adding up. Any time I sat down to write, I'd stop myself. I'd think:

> *This isn't marketable.*
> *This isn't funny.*
> *This won't sell.*
> *There are three other projects just like this.*

It was like I knew too much about how the sausage was made and who made it. This world I'd admired for my entire life was too close for comfort—too close for me to be creative with it. But I couldn't admit that to myself and I thought, *Well, maybe I'm meant to be on the producing or marketing side of things.*

So I did the dues paying, the impossible task doing, and the random errand running. *Joe lost his goggles. We think they look somewhat like this. Find them.* Over multiple years, I went from Lionsgate Films (they bought *The Hunger Games* while I was there) to Walt Disney Animation Studios (just as *The Princess and the Frog* was coming out), and later to a brand-new team at the time called Franchise Management at The Walt Disney Studios (as Tim Burton's *Alice in Wonderland* was releasing in theaters around the world).

I moved from an assistant up to a coordinator, a very big, multi-year accomplishment in the film industry. (I'd regularly meet people who would spend five or six years working as an assistant before they got a different title.) Through more years of sweat equity and opportunities, I was promoted to assistant manager, and my role changed to my "dream job" of writing and designing story presentations of live action and animated films.

I was doing it: making my dream happen. I was moving my way up the corporate ladder, dealing with the late nights and the politics, but one thing continued no matter the career milestones I reached: commuting car rides filled with tears of frustration.

For years, I had told everyone in my life that I wanted to be a creative force in the movie business. Yet, I knew in my heart of hearts, even after getting my biggest promotion ever, that things were off. This path just didn't make me happy the way I thought it would. By all accounts and on paper, I should have been ecstatic. But I wasn't.

To free myself from this, it was not only okay, but it was necessary to be able to rewrite my dream. But at the time I didn't know that because, like a lot of us, I felt trapped by "the one path." Maybe you've heard about it. It's time to know what it really is.

"The One Path" Is Bullshit

If you thought you had this career and life thing figured out until now, you're probably very familiar with the idea of "the one path." It's that unspoken recipe for success and happiness that we all know. Every industry has one that everybody pledges their allegiance to.

The basic life version goes something like: get amazing grades, go to an impressive college, go to grad school or professional school, or run a big business. *Oh!*—and don't forget to get married and have kids if you want to (one day) be happy and successful.

The future surgeon needs to crush every science class in undergraduate, go to a top medical school, do a competitive residency, and then snag a prestigious fellowship in order to (one day) be happy and successful.

The future film development executive needs to do big studio internships, earn an impossible-to-get job at the best talent agency you can, work as an assistant for multiple years, jump to a studio and work as an assistant again for multiple years, then get promoted. Then finally—*one day*—you'll ultimately be happy and successful, right?

Other industries have their narratives that everyone subscribes to; maybe you know some of them firsthand.

And here's the deal:

> *"The one path" is what people tell you that you have to do to "make it."*

"The one path" is what keeps you always trying to move on to the "next step" that everyone agrees will lead you to happiness and success.

"The one path" is what haunts you, and makes you feel like you'll never be happy and successful if you're not walking it.

"The one path" is a story that we all tell ourselves and compare ourselves to.

And it's time for you to know, loud and clear, once and for all: *The notion of "the one path" is total bullshit.*

There's More Than Just
"The One Path" to Success

In 2009, I attended a Duke alumni event on the Fox studio lot. It was pretty epic going behind the scenes and seeing the sets of big TV shows and films. In a crowded theater, surrounded by hundreds of my fellow alums, I got the opportunity to ask a question of the panel that included famous cinematographer and Duke alum Robert Yeoman *(Moonrise Kingdom, Rushmore)*.

I asked the panel, "How do you get started when you're fresh out of school and have just moved to Hollywood? Is there any other path than working at a talent agency?"

I can't remember what advice they gave exactly, but here's what I do remember: being accosted by a junior film development executive during the mixer following the panel. She came up to me and began to berate me about the question I'd asked. She stressed that the only way to get anywhere in the film industry was to work at a talent agency first and that I shouldn't be trying to skip that step.

All right, fair play. I asked her how she got her start. Apparently, she worked for a producer as an assistant and worked her way up from there. *She* had never worked for a talent agency. So why was she so insistent, bordering on irate, toward me?

"The one path."

"The one path" is the lie we're all telling ourselves about how success has to happen.

My experience with this woman wasn't unusual. In fact, it is quite common in Hollywood networking. Some of the advice you may always hear about the entertainment industry is that, no matter who you are, you've got to go work at a talent agency *first*. It's commonly referred to as the best place to start learning and making connections to grow your career, and it's not bad advice. It is a great way to do both of those things.

However, working at an agency first is not the *only* way to climb the Hollywood ladder. I got my first gig at a studio (Lionsgate) as a paid "executive" internship working as the second assistant for the president of the company. I know some people who came directly into major studios as temps, and others who simply happened to be in the right place at the right time and got a break. There is not one path; there are many.

Whatever you're facing, I encourage you to look around and consider the advice people give you as well as the path they've *actually* taken. The two don't often line up.

Consider your friends and family, or even look at famous people you admire. Their career "paths" are often atypical. Legendary chef Julia Child started her career in *advertising* for a home furnishings company called W. & J. Sloane and was ultimately fired for gross insubordination. Next stop? She became a world-traveling spy for the United States during World War II in 1941. She only began taking cooking lessons when she and her husband moved to France in 1948. Though it took her the better part of a decade to do it on her own terms, she went on to become one of the world's best-known and respected chefs, TV personalities, and cookbook authors.

It's not that strange to start in a different place than where you end up. What that should start to reinforce for you is that the concept of "the one path" is total crap. And that's a really liberating thing, because you're not going to be a failure if you stop following it. You're just going to be making your own way.

If you're going to try something new and rewrite your dream, stay the course when you meet these naysayers. No matter what industry you're in, you're going to have to deal with people like that development exec at the Duke event. They are going to tell you that you need to follow the steps. They are going to be the strangers who lecture you at networking events, people you meet for coffee, and professors who chastise you for thinking, feeling, or acting differently. They tell you that you need "the one path" because they are uncomfortable with the possibility that "the one path" could be bullshit.

Consider this about these "path patrollers": If "the one path" isn't real and it's just a construct we've invented, then what will that mean for their career? For their choices? For their apparent successes and failures? They've been acting from fear of the uncertainty and insecurity—most likely—throughout their career. You're challenging that if you challenge the concept of "the one path" to success.

Uncertainty, unknown—these are the things "the one path" distracts from and the things that unsettle us.

They—those who are uncomfortable with change and giving yourself permission to take risks—are afraid of uncertainty. So just know that whenever you get told there's a certain and "only" way to do things to get what you want. We'll explore this in Chapter 9, when I get into why people will surprise you.

CHAPTER 2

DOUBT:
*"Will I ever get to a life
that I love?"*

PERMISSION:

YOUR STORY WILL MAKE SENSE IN THE END (PROMISE)

We're Too Close
to Our Own Stories

I should tell you something as we're getting to know each other: I've been known to make people cry.

Let me explain. In my business as a brand creator, I help small business owners get outside of their own head about their value and their strengths. It's the core of the work I do: seeing someone's story and strengths where they can't, and giving them tangible ways in a logo, a tagline, or a website to share that value with ideal clients and customers.

During brand projects, I always make a point to verbally present their business's "Brand Voice Guide" to them. I read aloud their "About" story, a positioning statement, and even their 30-second elevator pitch, so they can actually experience it. I used to just email this document for their review, but I learned a few years ago that presenting it live to people can be incredibly powerful for them.

The thing about your "About" story or your positioning statement is that it's never going to be read in your voice. It's always going to be read by prospective customers or clients. So when I perform it for them, it allows my clients to get out of their own head—if only for a few minutes. And after reading "About" stories in particular, I've had a few of my clients cry happy tears. This said, the first time it happened, I was a little worried.

I was on the phone with Tiffany, a wedding planner in Durham. I had just finished reading and the line was quiet. Then, I could hear her choking back tears. *Oh no. Is she crying?*

I asked if she was okay and Tiffany shared with me, with joy in her voice, "It all makes sense. I never thought my career made sense like this, and you showed me how it all adds up! It all adds up."

Tiffany wasn't crying because my writing was so great. She was touched because she could see that her work had real value, and that all of her career twists and turns had all had purpose after all. She could finally see herself and her life in a beautiful light. For me, moments like this make the work I do the most rewarding thing I could ever imagine.

Tiffany's not alone. She was just the first client I've made cry this way. I've watched so many of my clients tear up upon hearing how their story adds up: how it makes sense and qualifies them to help others by way of their goods or services. I've made both men and women cry, across all kinds of industries. One thing that this always makes clear to me: We all have value, yet we all struggle with seeing it in ourselves.

I continue to learn that as individuals, we're not great judges of our potential, ability, or value. We are reluctant to give ourselves credit or feel that we can do so objectively. I think it's part of the reason why we're unlikely to give ourselves permission. We're all too close to our own stories to truly appreciate them. That's one of the reasons I do what I do and it's a major reason I've written *Permission to Try* for you.

If you have ever felt like your story doesn't make sense, consider that you might be too close to the action. If I've discovered anything in writing and presenting more than 50 of these "Brand Voice Guides" in the past five years, it's this: Your story is powerful, and it's going to make sense in the end. I promise.

You Can Only Tell
Your Story Backward

As you debate trying something new in your life or career, remember that you can't see how things are going to add up when you're smack dab in the middle of everything.

I remember crying my eyes out, feeling stuck in my job at Lionsgate Films. It was my first official film industry job out of college. I was working as a second assistant to the president of the company. It was supposed to be a six-month stint. From there, the notion was that I'd have an opportunity to promoted.

That six-month mark coincided with March 2009. If that time sounds familiar, you may remember there was massive unemployment across the country. Moreover, an infamous corporate raider named Carl Icahn was in the middle of trying to take over Lionsgate. It wasn't a climate to move forward at most companies, and in particular where I was.

I was feeling lost as I started job searching, internally and externally. I couldn't catch a break and started to feel like my role was never going to lead me to a meaningful career. I was sharing my frustration with my then-boyfriend/now-husband, Gus, who reminded me of Allison Shearmur, one of my first mentors in the film industry.

Small in stature and fond of calling many "Cookie" as a term of endearment, Alli was a powerful female force in the entertainment industry. A well-respected executive and producer, she was the president of production at Lionsgate when I was there. I admired her greatly and was appreciative of the times she'd trust me to cover her desk or invite me into her office to ask me how she could help me grow my career.

In many ways, I thought I wanted to be Alli someday. And Gus knew that. He pointed out that when Alli was coming up in the film industry, years before she'd reached such major status, she would have had no idea how one opportunity would lead to the next or how a setback would still get her to this great place she'd one day be.

"That's the thing," he said. "Alli will always only be able to tell the great story in hindsight. And so will you."

And so will you. We can never know where the twists and turns and uncertainty will lead us. We can only tell the story of major changes in our lives or careers after they've happened. We can only leap and trust that the story will make sense and happen how it was always supposed to.

Alli passed away in 2018 at the age of 54 while I was writing this book and just after I wrote this chapter. If I needed a more powerful reminder to keep going with the challenge of writing this book and to trust it will all work out, it's being reminded of her legacy. I've seen the impact she's had on so many people I know directly and been moved to think of the thousands more she reached through her films (including the Star Wars film *Solo*, which is dedicated to her memory).

I also get to remember, fondly, that Alli couldn't have known where her story would lead her through an incredible career; she simply had to live and write the story to find out.

And so will I, and so will you.

Reading a screenplay at my desk at Lionsgate in 2009.
Alli's office was just around the corner from my cubicle.
(Photo by Robyn Marshall)

Value What Others See in You

While I've been writing this book, I've been facing a challenge that has had me wishing the darn thing was finished so I'd have some sort of handy guide on how to keep moving through change. That challenge has been infertility.

I'm in the middle of a years-long struggle with infertility. You might be in the middle of a completely different challenge. Maybe you're dealing with a micromanaging boss, or riding the rollercoaster of a bad relationship, or facing something in your life that seems to keep taking the wind out of your sails.

Whatever we face, we can have ongoing things in our lives that keep us feeling defeated and unable to see our own worth. That's what infertility has become for me. If you are part of the one in eight couples in the United States who faced it, or have friends or family who have, you may already know what it's like. I've heard infertility described as an "invisible disability," regularly recurring grief that is comparable to having a major medical illness, and a marathon that you never know when it will end.

If you are a positive person, as I generally am, it really begins to weigh on you when month after month for years nothing happens, no matter what you do, how much money you spend, or how many vitamins you take. There's only so much hope I can reset sometimes; there's only so much strength I have.

My business has been flourishing through most of the three-plus years we've been trying for children. So behind the scenes of that outward success, having a baby has been my focus and the thing I just can't figure out, or plan, or be strategic about. It's the worst nightmare for someone like me who's a planner and action-taker by nature. At this point, if it's going to happen for us, it'll happen, and I'm pretty confident that I have no clue when that will be.

I have to say, this cycle of hope turned to disappointment, and the possibly unending search for answers and results, has worn on me. It has made me feel weak and like a failure, because my body can't do what so many others' bodies can so easily.

I have good days, but I also have pretty awful ones. One such day this year, I called my dad while I was driving to a help host a workshop. I was not in a good place. Maybe you've had moments like this. Basically, I was feeling like I was a little girl again: crying to my daddy and asking that he promise to make everything better. It takes a lot to get anyone to that point: where you can't go any farther and that all you want in the world is for your parents to just fix everything. That's where I was.

"Daddy, rescue me. I'm drowning. I don't know how to do this. I'm terrified of the unknown."

Dad listened to me cry and get angry, then frustrated with the journey I've been going through. When I was finished bawling my eyes out and had given up at his feet, he said something I never expected.

He said, "Annie, you are tough. And you need to know, you are bigger than all of your problems."

You are tough.

What?! On every email survey and on every personality test I've ever taken (even *Which Muppet are you?* on BuzzFeed), I choose "creative" to describe myself. "Artsy." "Positive." "Innovative." Never, ever "tough." I was the kid who "ran" a 15-minute mile as a personal best. I cried on a Jet Ski (yes, a Jet Ski) on my honeymoon. I never, ever think of myself as tough.

But there was my dad, with me coming to him and literally begging him to solve my problems, pointing out something I never give myself credit for: I *am* tough.

Though this isn't my go-to descriptor of myself, I find that when I look closely, it's surprisingly true. I am tough. I have been through a lot and I keep standing up and trying again, no matter the outcome or how much harder it gets. But I hadn't been giving myself credit for that at all. I needed my dad to see it and to remind me of it.

"You are bigger than all of your problems."

At the time, I was wanting to be rescued and again, Dad reminded me I am bigger than what I am facing. I am capable of tackling what feels so impossible because I am bigger than everything going on. I couldn't see it that way; I needed him to show it to me.

And it keeps happening to me. A few months back, I had coffee with my friend, calligrapher Maghon Taylor of All She Wrote Notes. (She's famous on the internet, I'm pretty sure.) Out of nowhere, she gave me a simple and tremendous gift: She just said, "Annie, I am just so proud of you. You've had a really hard couple of years. You've created this business out of nothing and it's made everything possible."

I never really think that I've "had a really hard couple of years" or that, thanks to my business, we can do big financial things like treating infertility out-of-pocket and sending my husband, Gus, to physical therapy school in 2019. But when she said that, I felt like I could give myself permission to be proud and embrace what accomplishments have happened, even in the hard times.

Since these conversations, I've been in a better headspace as our journey through infertility continues. I've started an "Attitude of Gratitude" playlist on Amazon music with '90s favorites and happy songs. I've begun writing 15 things I am grateful for that happened that day in a gratitude journal every night. After a few months of this, I'm finding that I am scanning the world for the positive more often and feeling less lost, less like a failure, and more appreciative of all that I do have.

The people in your life see you in an entirely different light than you will ever, *ever* see yourself. Ask them for their help and their perspective, and ask them to coffee. When you are struggling to give yourself credit, you will find that there's so much more to *who you are* than you can see. And when they help you see it, I hope that you can find a way to own it.

That's what I'm trying to do these days by staying tough, knowing that I am bigger than my problems, and appreciating what all my hard work has made possible—even in a difficult, uncertain season of life.

Me and Dad. Circa 1990 or last week, can't remember. Hard to tell.
(Photo by Barbara Saunders)

Give Yourself Some Credit

As we've seen throughout this chapter, it can be tough to make sense of your story. It's especially hard when you aren't giving yourself credit for the person you are and what you've already accomplished—even if your plans haven't worked out how you'd hoped so far.

It can be easy to always be looking ahead—to the next step, the next big promotion, the next big sale in your business. In his TED Talk, "The Happy Secret to Better Work," psychologist and author Shawn Achor refers to this as us "pushing happiness over the cognitive horizon." Generally explained, we don't sit in the "now" and intentionally feel and enjoy happiness. We don't give ourselves credit for our greatness and what we've already accomplished. We are usually chasing success and happiness instead of embracing it and using it for momentum forward. *CELEBRATE!!!*

As a small business owner, I like to say that most days, my business runs on confidence. You can imagine I definitely have hard days when I am not feeling very confident or feeling tapped into my own value. Maybe it's human nature, but I think it's hard to give yourself credit for what you are capable of and what you have accomplished. It's challenging to be objective about it, and it's tough to keep up a positive attitude all the time. And the reality is that you're going to second-guess yourself like 400 times at least (before the week is out), but you do have value.

You may think, *What have I done that's had an impact?* Well, maybe there are other questions you should be asking—questions that have a way of helping you quantify value. Turn the page and try this out.

**TIME TO GIVE YOURSELF
SOME CREDIT**

HAVE HANDY: *Pen / pencil and a sheet of paper (or notebook)*

This is the first of several exercises spread throughout the book. These bite-size adventures (most just requiring pen and paper) should make it easier to see progress and take meaningful action in your life.

For this one, answer the following questions from your gut:

- *How many people have I helped through my job or business?*
- *How many things have I created that others have used, enjoyed, or needed?*
- *How many relationships have I made positive contributions to?*
- *How many coffees have I had with people to help them get started?*
- *How many things have I had the courage to try?*
- *How many people have I been there for during difficult times?*

Keep going and brainstorm what other questions you could ask yourself. Try to put numbers and quantities against what you've done, and I think you'll have a harder time not giving yourself credit for what you've done thus far.

—

We are always so focused on the next big thing and those "shared" societal definitions of success that it can be very odd to stop and look more closely at our present and our past. But remember: You have thousands of interactions a year with people, so odds are that during some of them you are adding value to others' lives, and your own.

Another thing you can do to literally give yourself credit is start keeping what I call a "Professional Life Journal." Wouldn't it be amazing if you could go back and read the story of your career? That's the idea. Imagine a diary that documents your professional life instead of your personal life. If you keep it for a career, you can record your career wins, interviews, manager struggles, and reflections. If you keep it as a business owner, you can document new clients, growth spurts (larger packages booked for the first time, etc.), business challenges you've overcome, milestones like reaching X number of clients or sales, and more.

The trick is to write in it regularly (I do mine monthly) and review it often. You can use a paper journal or do what I do: start a Google document and send yourself a monthly calendar reminder email to update it.

Because I keep this professional life journal, I can trace the peaks and valleys of my business all the way back to 2012, when it was just a nebulous, nutty idea. I can see where I started and what I've built it into. I can see the storms I weathered, and the growth that happened after the rains passed. I have a way to talk to my past self and do what is so hard for anyone to do: give myself credit and feel good about the work I'm doing.

Whether you answer these questions, start a journal, or just take time to think about what it is that you've done well and contributed to the world, my hope for you is simply that you do something.

You are too awesome not to realize that you're awesome!

FREE RESOURCE

Get my free template for starting
your own professional life journal
at *permissiontotry.com*.

CHAPTER 3

GO BEYOND "DO WHAT YOU LOVE"

There's More to
"Do What You Love"

"Do what you love" should have a little asterisk on it and a bit more explanation. Here's how I see it:

> Do what you love*
> *and what you are good at
> that adds value to other people

It's not enough to simply "do what you love." It needs to serve your talents, and it needs to add value (ideally in a way that people can and would pay you for).

To me, this is the formula to rewarding work and it explains exactly why my big, sexy Hollywood job wasn't fulfilling. It was something I loved, and something I was good at, but it didn't add enough value to other people to make it *rewarding* for me.

I grew up believing "do what you love" and using it as a north star to guide my career and life choices. I believe we all want to do something with our lives that we love—something we're passionate about. But I have to tell you from my experience getting my dream job, and then realizing that it was just a job and not a whole life: I've had to revise my definition of "do what you love."

It was a few years ago, while I was still at Disney, that I began to realize there's a lot more to it than just "do what you love." In working on reinventing myself, I began considering what my life might look like at the end of my career—sometime when I'm 65 or 70. This is when I first encountered the great advice of author-entrepreneurs Lara Casey and Richie Norton.

I first met Lara Casey when I attended the Making Things Happen conference in March 2013, smack dab in the middle of rethinking my film industry career. Known for inventing the famous goal-setting system of Powersheets and her books, *Make it Happen* and *Cultivate,* Lara has taught me so much about naming and facing fears, as well as the critical value of visualizing what I want my future to look like. One exercise at the conference had us all lying on the floor of the Carolina Inn, eyes closed, imagining what our lives might look like in five years, no matter how impossible that vision seemed. A lot of my initial vision came true, down to the townhouse we live in with my home office just to the left of the door! Back then and even now—Lara always inspires me to move and grow personally with intention.

I discovered Richie initially through his book *The Power of Starting Something Stupid.* One of the tremendous lessons I got from his book was doing something Richie calls "The Bezos Test" (named for visionary entrepreneur and Amazon CEO Jeff Bezos). Simply put, Richie describes this as facing opportunities and asking yourself, "Will I regret it when I'm 80?" The notion of the test and exercise comes from Jeff Bezos's true career story in 1998, when he was debating whether to leave a great gig on Wall Street to take a risk and start Amazon.

On this advice and with Lara's encouragement on my mind, I literally undertook "The Bezos Test" that Richie presents in *The Power of Starting Something Stupid.* I made a list of what I'd hoped to have accomplished by the end of my life and career, so I could make decisions now based on that. In this process, I took time to think about what I would like my life to look like near the end.

What would I have hoped to have done? What about if I hadn't gotten to?

Surprisingly, these emerged as the most important ᵔ my list:

1. Run a business that makes a difference in people's lives
2. Write a book that helps people
3. Have a family

It was eye-opening. I considered how I might feel if I stayed in my current "dream job" or ones like it for the rest of my career. I could see clearly that I'd regret staying in Corporate America. I wanted to accomplish more in my life than that job or other industry jobs would have led me to. And while I loved many aspects of the job I had, and it was the very picture of success to many people, it wasn't making enough of an impact on other people's lives for it to be my entire life's work.

Though I worked on major films, I wasn't changing the films themselves. Movies were getting made whether or not I was in the picture. That left making my bosses happy as the chief by-product of my work. I don't know if you've ever had a boss before, but even with the best ones, what happens once you make them happy? Five minutes later, they're unhappy about something else and you're off to solve that problem. For me, that wasn't enough of a rewarding reason to continue. Stepping back and considering what I would want my career as a whole to look like woke me up to my professional desire to change lives. And it made me realize—I was going to have to do my own thing to make that happen. "Do what you love" was simply not going to be enough of a compass for me.

..'hether you are able live your passion as a career or have to work a more practical job to support yourself and/or others, I think we all want to feel like what we've done with our lives has mattered to other people. You're trying to find something that you love to do that's also going to add meaning to the world. It's something you are uniquely good at, you can add value to, and is rewarding to you. If you do have to have a more practical job or career, think of this as what to do whenever you are able to have free patches of time to do something with your passions.

Whatever the case, be mindful of the big picture and what matters to you about it—and especially *who* matters to you. Funnily enough, it turns out "do what you love" is not just about you: It's about the people you want to impact. When you realize that, you may find that your passion is more than just what you personally want, but also what you can give back. It's been my experience that this is where you find the good stuff.

If you're not sure what your next career dream may be yet, you can get started by doing one of my favorite exercises to go beyond "do what you love."

| TAKE ACTION EXERCISE | A TANGIBLE WAY TO START FINDING A NEW DIRECTION |

HAVE HANDY: *Pen / pencil and a sheet of paper (or notebook)*

Make three lists next to each other on one sheet of paper or in your notebook.

1. What I love
2. What I'm good at
3. What I loved to do as a kid *(See the next story for more context.)*

Now look across these lists and see if you can find
that offer value to other people—ideally ways that th
and be able to pay for.

Here's what the start of my lists would look like. Yours could be shorter or longer, as you'd like and find helpful.

WHAT I LOVE	WHAT I'M GOOD AT	WHAT I LOVED TO DO AS A KID
Movies	Writing	Performing
Disney	Graphic design	Going to the movies
Writing	Telling stories	Making gifts for others
Being creative	Branding	Giving speeches
Muppets	Strategy	Art class
Making people happy	Self-management	Helping friends & family
Public speaking	Starting things	Writing parodies & stories
Cookie dough	Building presentations	Creating kids newsletters
Spending time with people who inspire me	Seeing potential and strengths in others	Designing t-shirts for events

You can see that I love cookie dough, and I'm pretty good at eating it, and I even loved it as a kid—but dude, it doesn't offer any value to me to make eating cookie dough a career dream.

You can also see that I love being creative and spending time with people who inspire me; I'm good at seeing people's strengths and potential, telling stories, and doing writing and graphic design; and I always used to create things for other people as a kid (like branded gifts and newsletters). This is one set of intersections that has led me to the work I do now for amazing small business owners, telling their stories through clear and engaging business names, logos, taglines, websites, and more.

When you do your own lists, consider this: *What intersections can you see? Are they any you hadn't considered before?*

For further learning, consider researching the Japanese concept of "ikigai" that delves far deeper into a related idea of finding intersections of your values and talents to find your purpose.

FREE RESOURCE

Share your work or grab a free template for this exercise at *permissiontotry.com*.

It's a Version of
What You Loved as a Kid

If you're not sure about your new plan and purpose, you're not alone. No matter your age, it's daunting to feel like you still haven't discovered what you're meant to do. One of the most freeing things I've ever read about this comes from author Jon Acuff. He writes in *Quitter* that the way to finding your purpose is not a process of discovery. Instead, it's a "process of recovery." He explains, "You don't ask the bottomless 'What do I want to do with my life?' but instead, 'What have I done in my life that I loved doing?'"

We read *Quitter* in the season that Gus and I were entertaining the crazy idea of giving up our dream careers. One of the things that was stopping me and filling me with fear was having no clue what I'd do instead. *What was my purpose?* But reading Acuff's advice was eye-opening. What if what I was meant to do next had been a part of my story all along? What if all I needed to do was go back—even as far back as my childhood—and simply look more closely? If my purpose was already there, I didn't need to fear finding the answers. They would be there for me to recover.

Thinking about identifying a new purpose as an act of recovery was another form of permission I needed. It was something that told me, "It's okay. You've already been where you're meant to go." So I started to get back in touch with the person I was as a kid and a teenager. The question became "What have I always loved to do?"

If you're anything like me, it can be hard to get into that headspace when you've been pursuing a big career. Being super-career-driven can make a funny thing happen: You can forget all the things you once loved to do because you have become so focused on being

41

professional and ambitious to "make it." That's what had happened to me.

By the time I was 16, I'd "picked" writing in the film industry as my dream. And because it was my "one path," I knew what I had to do: march forward for the next decade, completely focused on what it would take to get there. Internships, assistant jobs, coordinator gigs, and Corporate America led me further and further from the kid I used to be and the things I loved to do. The ironic thing about this path is that it wasn't even creative—the quality that had brought me to the party in the first place. Instead, I often was spending 90% of my time on everything but creative work: booking meetings, finding conference rooms, dealing with people and politics. And I was about a million miles from the Annie who was always creating things to add value to other people. In fact, without realizing it, I'd gone entire years without making much of anything at all.

I'd all but forgotten the roots of who I used to be until I read a screenplay that was floating around town, *The Muppet Man* by Christopher Weekes. It's Jim Henson's life story, told with Muppets and all. In a short two hours, I finished the script with tears running down my face, so moved by Jim Henson, what he created, and how he left us all too soon (he passed away in 1990). It woke me up to the things I've always loved outside of the film industry. I was reminded of my deep love of silly things like The Muppets, characters who'd been my friends since the days of watching *Muppet Babies* and going to "Muppet Vision 3D" on our annual trips to Walt Disney World. It gave me a new appreciation for what Jim Henson created and the impact it had on kids like me. It made me feel like a kid again—and made me remember what it was to create something meaningful.

It was a tipping point for me that began to wake me up to the little pieces of myself I'd been leaving behind in pursuit of my corporate career. It would take years of twists, turns, and reflections to get to what I'm doing now, many of which I'm sharing throughout this book. But looking back, I can say confidently that Jon Acuff was spot on. Though the light bulb didn't go off immediately, finding my current mission (as I'd describe it today) was absolutely a process of recovery. For me, a lot of it came from embracing the things that have always been true about me since I was a little girl.

I know now that my life's work has always been all about branding, helping people tell their story and doing what I can to empower others to chase their big dreams through speaking and writing. The funny thing is that when I look to my childhood, branding and marketing were so much of what I did. I just didn't know *that's* what those things were called! I called them newsletters I co-wrote with my childhood best friend, Tricia, called "Totally Kids Only" or the senior year t-shirts I designed for "The Ellen Olson Brooks 'Writing Center' for Seniors that Can't Write Good (and Want to Learn to Do Other Stuff Good Too)." At the time, I didn't know I was making logos or that creating the look of a website was a job; they were things I enjoyed doing because they were creative and made the people I loved happy. I wasn't aware that giving speeches for honor society and graduation, or writing parody scripts and songs to celebrate my classmates, could be actual *jobs*. I mean, get serious!

But there it all was, all along. Finding ways to turn those skills and interests into a career has made me feel like I've come home to myself. And it's all the more reason that my first dream, while valuable, was only part of a journey that has helped me come full circle.

It's had me thinking that picking just one dream—doing all that it takes to climb the career ladder—maybe isn't the way we're meant to do it. Maybe it limits us and keeps us from embracing all the facets of who we are and who we've been all along. Maybe it's why my first dream didn't work out as I planned and that your first, second, or even third dream might not be working out, either.

Meshing the things I loved to do as a kid with the ways I can add value as an entrepreneur has made me feel like a more grounded person. It's given me a broader and more "me" purpose. And with this, I've realized it's silly to think we are all meant to do "just one thing" or pick just "one path."

We are each so much more than our one big, obvious career interest. We are not meant to do just one job or have just one dream our whole lives. Maybe it's okay to change your life and redefine your purpose, and to have that happen more than once. And maybe we'll find the best new directions in the things that make us feel at home—the things that you make you feel like a kid again.

TAKE ACTION EXERCISE

BEGIN YOUR OWN
PROCESS OF RECOVERY

HAVE HANDY: *Pen / pencil and a sheet of paper (or notebook)*

In this extension of the previous exercise in this chapter, dive deeper into what you loved as a kid.

1. Clear your space.
2. Set a timer for **25 minutes**.

3. Do a brainstorm around the topic "things I loved to do as a kid."
4. Enjoy the remembering. Write down things big and small.
5. After 25 minutes, circle the things that might have real-life equivalents of things people would pay you for (as an entrepreneur or as an employee).
6. Repeat as needed, and encourage yourself to be thinking about the person you've always been (not just the person you feel like you've had to be from a career standpoint).

The school t-shirt logo I created before I really knew what graphic design was. (Photo by the author)

Create Opportunities
for the Career You Want

As I've been sharing, it takes time, reflection, and, as you'll soon learn, *action*, to get to a life and career that feel completely you. What do you do in the meantime while you're sorting it all out? Get out there and create opportunities for the kind of career you want to happen. Start with what you know *now* and trust that the rest will happen if you're putting yourself into the world.

So much of my career started and blossomed beyond my wildest imagination just by throwing out my shingle and saying, "Hey world, this is what I can do!"

It was November 2012. I'd just spent the past year or so prior planning our June 16, 2012, wedding. The wedding and its 20+ DIY projects had turned out to be an incredible creative outlet for me that, in and of itself, reminded me how much I missed making things and using my creative skill sets. For the wedding party, I crafted little wooden Polaroid bouquet pins for the bridesmaids' bouquets, each featuring a picture of me with the bridesmaid.

At the time I was working at Disney and feeling pretty disempowered. I was low man on the totem pole in terms of movies that I was assigned to and felt pretty out of control of my own career destiny. I decided I would start a blog on the side as a way to have an online shop where I sold these wooden bouquet pins. It would be a creative outlet—a tiny piece of the internet that I could own. I didn't think I'd ever go full-time, but I remember thinking, *Wow! This is going to be awesome. I'm going to make these things for so many weddings.*

I created wooden Polaroid bouquet pins for all my bridesmaids and for my own bouquet. Mine featured a favorite picture of me and my mom.
(Photo by Brett & Jessica Photography, brettjessica.com)

The set of wooden bouquet pins I created to sell on my online store, anniemade.
(Photo by the author)

So, true to my "Annie taking action" intensity, I learned WordPress in a weekend, named it anniemade, launched, and began blogging three times a week. That was a lot of new to get used to, but it was a fun adventure. What happened a few months later as a result is something I could never have predicted.

I had shared our wedding invitations online as a blog post in the hopes of promoting my handmade pin business. Our invitations were story booklets that told our love story, complete with adorable baby pictures and the wedding invitation itself. I talked all about how I wrote and designed the invites to be really "us" and tell our love story.

One day in 2013, I got an email because of that blog post. It was from a bride named Bridget. She lived in New York City and was getting married the following month in Savannah, Georgia. She didn't ask about buying the pins. Instead, she said she loved how I told our love story in our wedding invitations and asked if I could write and design her wedding programs.

Me? A graphic designer? And a *writer* of wedding programs? Does anyone even do that professionally? Well, as of Bridget's email, I did. She was my first client for using my skills of writing and design to tell someone's story. And I wasn't even marketing myself this way! Without realizing it, Bridget had seen incredible potential in what I was doing and she launched the ship that would one day become my current business and career: Greatest Story.

It was what I did for Bridget's wedding that helped me understand that I wanted to help real people tell their story as a job. Hers was an example I could point to when I realized that my "dream" job in Hollywood wasn't really changing lives. The notion of using writing and design to create wedding invitations, event decorations, and business branding was all, in many ways, born with her email. And that'd be an email I wouldn't have even had without the luck and kindness of our favorite search engine, Google. Like a chain reaction, anniemade and opportunities like this led me to leaving my career in film and starting Greatest Story Creative in October 2013. It played a big part in me realizing that I wanted to somehow make my entire career about helping real people like you tell your story.

But sometimes I wonder: What if I hadn't put myself out there and started that blog? Or opened that shop with the pins? Would it have happened? Would someone like Bridget have found me? Would I have ever realized this path on my own?

I'll never know. But I do know two things: 1) I'm really grateful that I jumped in and got out in the world, showing what I could do even though I didn't have a plan, and 2) I never sold a single one of those damn bouquet pins that got me to start the whole thing! It just goes to show you that you can never know what's coming next, but you can keep trying on what you do know *now*.

The front of our storybook wedding invitations.
It featured silhouettes that related to our love story—like London (where we met),
the In-N-Out arrow, and even a Netflix envelope (before the days of streaming!).
(Photo by Brett & Jessica Photography, brettjessica.com)

The inside featured an eight-page love story about our heroes, Annie and Gus.
(Photo by Brett & Jessica Photography, brettjessica.com)

PART TWO

Embrace Change and Take Action

CHAPTER 4

DOUBT:

"But other people can do big things. I'm not like them."

PERMISSION:

**ACTION
BEATS
TALENT**

55

Years and Action Make You
an "Overnight Success"

My husband, Gus Franceschi: future physical therapist and all-around good guy.
(Photo by the author)

This is the picture of a guy who was just got accepted to physical therapy school. Elon gets 800–900 applications a year for 46 seats, so he's just found out he's officially one of the top 6% of applicants that are offered admission. And this is also the picture of a guy who's been awarded a scholarship that will cover 15% of his entire degree.

He's awesome and this is extraordinary. But maybe you look at a story like this and think, "Well, he must have something I don't, to be able to do all that. It must be talent."

You need to know that there's so much in this picture of my husband, Gus, that you can't see. You can't see the 10-year career in the film industry that came before it. You can't see the confusion and stress that come with finding out your first career dream wasn't what it was cracked up to be. You can't see the multi-year journey of student loans, part-time jobs, and time he had to put in at 23 years old to go back to school and finish his bachelor's degree.

You don't learn about the full-time jobs he worked so we could stay out of debt, so I could be an entrepreneur with minimal risk. You don't know the emotional sacrifices he made to keep jobs he didn't like so we could do things like buy a house and begin trying to start a family. And you don't see the time, in the middle of this road, that he got laid off, my clients dried up for a spell, and everything got thrown out the window for six weary months.

Maybe most powerfully, you can't see the 2,000+ hours Gus worked that directly made this picture possible:

- *The 11 science courses taken on the side over the course of three years*

- *The nine schools he had to attend and get transcripts from to qualify for admission*
- *The 100 shadowing hours he had to complete around a traditional 9–5 Monday–Friday job when most physical therapy firms keep the exact same hours*
- *The GRE test score he missed by just 1% and then had to retake*
- *The semesters he spent with our science-genius friends who kindly tutored him over Skype (Thanks, Dr. Mike and Harlan!)*
- *The tears over Chemistry I—so many tears*
- *And the dozens of meetings with me where we strategically worked together to figure out every requirement, grade, course, and more to make this moment possible*

Even in this picture, in the back of his head, he couldn't really celebrate fully because he had a Physics 2 exam the next morning! Yet, it is still a picture of success; there's just more to the story.

It is easy to look at others and think, *I can't do that. They are innately talented. They were born with opportunity and talents that I don't have.* But if Gus's picture should tell you anything, it's that we hold ourselves back when we write off talent as innate, and when we see others' success and assume it's not possible for us.

Gus and I have experienced that success doesn't come directly from opportunity or uncontrollable fate. It's a result of persistence—of action. And action will beat talent every time.

For as long as I can remember, my nana has liked to say, *"Anne was born with a gold star on her head."* I know this is her way of saying how proud she is of me. However, when she says it, I have mixed feelings. The thing is that saying I have "a gold star" on my head can imply to others that they can't be successful or talented, because I was innately born with my abilities.

I call this reaction "stargazing"—looking at others' success, talents, social media, and more and thinking, *Well, they have things I could never have, and they are things I could never be. They were born with a star on their head, so I might as well not try.*

And that's the danger. Too much stargazing means you don't try. You don't take action. You tell yourself a narrative that these stars are exceptional, extraordinary, unreachable. You tell yourself it's okay to be normal and not to shoot for them, because there is something special they have that's totally unobtainable.

I want you to succeed at whatever you want to do with your life, and I don't want anyone's success (or even perception of success) to hold you back from shining yourself. We admire amazing people and their meteoric success—but we don't stop to really see all the things they had to do to get there in the first place. We only see Z; we don't know what A, B, and C were along the way. *Because, remember Chapter 2 of this book: We can only tell our own success stories in hindsight.*

There are probably countless examples I could use, but let's use me— for Nana's sake, and since I'm a big action-taker. In celebrating the fifth-year anniversary of my business this year, I feel very lucky to have started and grown a career I love. I'm grateful that this business has changed many lives beyond my own. In the past five years, I've also become a professional speaker and have been growing that side of my career, creating signature events and speaking at conferences. It would be easy to look at this and miss the whole story—to simply say it's because of the star on my head.

But take a closer look:

- *For every speaking opportunity I do, there are at least 15 times as many emails I've sent into the universe pitching myself as a speaker that never ever get replied to.*
- *For every new client I book, there are several that say no or aren't a good fit.*
- *For every well-written newsletter or blog post I write for Greatest Story, there are those with embarrassing typos and the evenings when I was so behind on client work, I didn't write one at all.*
- *For every peak, there are valleys: late nights, confusion, missteps, and more.*

Even if you consider my previous career with Disney, that incredible experience only came after hustling to get unpaid internships, working a second assistant job, getting laid off, difficult job interviews, crying during my daily commute, and more.

Not everything I try works—far from it. In the past two years alone, I bombed hard at selling my first digital product, had to cancel my first DIY group brand coaching program due to low enrollment, and even accidentally poached my own sold-out live event audience by offering a webinar option *(a sizable number stopped coming at all for months because it felt like less of a special event—oops!).*

But over this same period of time, I've also tried a lot of things that have worked. I created an in-person, monthly workshop series in Durham called Branding with Annie that's sold out more than a dozen times and had more than 200 attendees over the past 18 months. This series has led to major local brand awareness for what I do and brought me dream clients. I also booked my biggest speaking gig ever (and my first one out of state) by quoting an outrageous number and backing it up with a bit of confidence and creativity. And I found a way to plan all of my marketing content for a full year ahead of time, so I've gotten to enjoy 12 months of not having to worry about what I'll talk about in my business newsletter.

So that's the real-real. I'll tell you again what makes all the difference in being successful. It's not talent; *it's unrelenting action.*

Unrelenting action comes in the form of things like:

- *Sending emails to pitch yourself,*
- *Having one-on-ones with others,*
- *Trying new things,*
- *Telling people what you're working on,*
- *Asking for help from someone you admire,*
- *Putting your name in the hat, and*
- *Showing up, even when you don't feel like it.*

American entertainer Eddie Cantor once said, *"It takes 20 years to make an overnight success."*

Action will trump quiet, inactive brilliance and talent every. single. time. We can't let others' highlight reels paralyze us and talk us into thinking we lack possibility and potential. We can't let not knowing what's coming in six months or a year stop us from trying something that sounds good for today. As Sheryl Sandberg says in *Lean In,* "Done is better than perfect." You don't have to strive for success or develop your talent for me, or for anyone else for that matter. You should always get out there and try for you.

- *Yes, talent matters.*
- *Yes, savvy matters.*
- *Yes, luck plays a role.*
- *But ACTION—action will always set you apart every time from everybody that's out there stargazing!*

You already have everything you need to succeed. You don't need to have been "born with a star on your head" to shine. Channel your own light and take action.

| TAKE ACTION EXERCISE | TRADE STARGAZING FOR REALIZING YOUR OWN POTENTIAL |

HAVE HANDY: *Pen / pencil and a sheet of paper (or notebook)*

- Make a list of the people you admire and think of as examples of extraordinary people whose success you think you could never achieve. They can be famous or they can be real people in your life.

- Research.

   For those who are famous, read their biography (or at least their Wikipedia page) and look for their whole story, not just the success you're already aware of. Take note of challenges they've overcome, unexpected failures or setbacks they've had, and when and how they took a lot of action in their lives and careers.

   For those you know personally, invite them to lunch or a phone call to ask them about their careers.

Ask questions like these:

- *Will you tell me about a time you failed?*
- *Did you always know what you wanted to do?*
- *What have been the hardest challenges you've faced?*
- *Have you ever felt lost on what to do with your career or your life?*

- Embrace this exercise and repeat it as often as you'd like. If you chose famous people the first time, do it with the people in your real life (who are probably easier to interview) the next time.

When you do this, my hunch is you'll find that many of the people you know and admire have rich stories that may not be all too different from your own. You may even find an appreciation for things you've got in your life that these people had to struggle to get.

My sincere hope is that you realize you have just as much potential to be among the stars you look to for inspiration. Maybe it can help you swap "Other people can be successful, but I can't" for "If they can do it, so can I."

Make Your Own Magic

If you're willing to embrace the idea that you have as much possibility in your life as those you admire, you're ready to hear one of the biggest secrets to success. It's actually not a secret at all. It's simply realizing that the world belongs to those who do things—"do-ers." To be a do-er is to make your own magic. When you become a do-er, the world belongs to you.

On any given day—at any given moment—you make a choice. You do or you don't. (You may remember what Yoda had to say about this, too.) History tells us, as far back as we can look, that the people who get remembered, *did*. They did something. They created something. They started something or said something. They took action.

While intellectually most of us know this, it's something that's easy to overlook. It's something that we don't consider when it comes to the pressures of our daily lives. Think about how you can sometimes feel in your job or your business.

When will they promote me?
Will they hire me?
Would someone ask me to speak?

If I've learned anything in my own story, it's that we cannot wait for the opportunities to come our way. We have to *do*. We have to make things happen. We don't have control over everything in our lives and we never will. However, we always have the ability to do something. Maybe it's something small that we've overlooked. Maybe it's something that will be hard, outside-the-box, or both. Whatever it is, the power of doing lies within us and no one else.

Consider the success of the blockbuster Broadway musical *Hamilton*. Known today for seemingly endless sold-out performances and outrageous ticket prices on Broadway and beyond, the show was written by its star, Lin-Manuel Miranda. It's the story of Alexander Hamilton and the founding of the American government. Miranda cast himself in the title role, incredibly mixed rap and hip-hop music with Broadway ballads, and cast his friends in the parts. Alexander Hamilton was played by Miranda, a Puerto Rican. Aaron Burr, Marquis de Lafayette, George Washington—all were played by African-Americans, many of whom were friends and frequent collaborators of Miranda's.

And it worked. It worked like no one could have ever anticipated. No casting director on the Great White Way would have ever cast diverse minorities in a story about our founding fathers. Miranda did. In fact, Miranda wrote the show that made that not only a possible choice, but a brilliant one.

In a skit for a Broadway Cares event called "Easter Bonnet" in 2016, the Broadway cast of *Fun Home* points out what makes this so special. The kids wrote and performed a parody of "Gee Officer Krupke!" from the Broadway classic *West Side Story*. (You can currently watch this amazingness at *vimeo.com/164477520*.)

Their parody version is called "Gee Mr. Miranda," and the whole thing's an adorable pitch for Lin-Manuel Miranda to write them a new hit show, since he's been so astronomically successful. Over the course of the song's lyrics, they share a major "a-ha" moment about Lin's story and the power of being a do-er. They point out that Lin-Manuel Miranda didn't wait for someone to write this once-in-a-lifetime, amazing show for him. Instead, he and his friends chose to "make their own magic." And in turn, the kids could and should do the same: write their own show—AKA make their own magic.

Make your own magic.

Record-breaking Broadway musicals don't write themselves. Great opportunities aren't destined to come our way. Change in our lives doesn't lead us where we want to go unless we get involved in some way. Sometimes it takes little changes. Other times, it takes big ones. And usually, it takes a lot of both that add up over time.

It's the doing that always makes change possible. So if you're looking for magic, realize you can always make your own. Become a do-er, and the world and its possibilities belong to you.

Don't Keep Your Dreams a Secret

If you want to make your own magic but feel intimidated to start, there's something simple you may be overlooking. Every day, you get at least one free and powerful opportunity to make your dream happen. You're running into someone, somewhere, and this chance is there, waiting for you to seize it. You may be looking right past it, and it's likely you're completely underestimating it.

What am I talking about?
You need to tell more people the next thing you want to try.

I don't mean what job you want next. I mean, tell people what new thing or dream you are currently thinking of trying out.

Maybe you are thinking of starting a jewelry business on the side.
 . . . or you're considering writing a book about baseball.
 . . . or you are fascinated by tech startups and are thinking of working at one someday.
 . . . or you're toying with going back to school to study interior design after doing a home renovation.

Whatever it is—personal, professional, entrepreneurial—it is critical that you take the step to tell other people and resist the urge to keep it a secret. *Why?* You may wonder and think:

- *But this idea is so early. I should probably figure it all out first before I tell anyone, so I don't look like an idiot.*
- *I'm not sure if it's what I want to do or commit to yet.*
- *What if it's stupid?*

If any of these reasons to keep your hopes a secret sound familiar, you're not alone. I deal with this, too. But I want you to realize that you could be missing major opportunities when others have no idea what you're working on or thinking about testing out.

Here's why this is so important: When you tell people about your dream, a magical thing tends to happen. People begin to help you make that dream a reality.

In my five years in Corporate America and five years as an entrepreneur so far, I can tell you that this is by far the single easiest and greatest step to success you can practice throughout your career. This is truly where both brand awareness and just plain old awareness begin.

Have you ever thought about what it might unlock when someone in your life is aware of what you're hoping to do? Maybe they will clip an article for you or introduce you to a friend that can help. Maybe they will make a powerful suggestion you have never considered or invite you to attend a game-changing event with them. This can happen especially with something newly forming in your world.

A crowdfunding platform like Kickstarter is completely built on this very idea. Entrepreneurs often share only the concept or prototype of what they want to do using their page on Kickstarter.com, and that early story can be enough to fund and launch the entire product or an entire company, to the tune of thousands or millions of dollars.

Perhaps we know the value of telling people intellectually, but putting it into practice can be intimidating. The barriers are real and big. So many of us are too scared or intimidated to do it—to simply give voice to what it is we are working on or dreaming about. And absolutely there are good reasons to keep some of your dreams, goals, and interests under your hat. There can be a "time and place" for things that you need to consider, especially if there's a worry or possibility of losing a job over something like having a side business. I don't mean for this to be blanket advice that applies 100% of the time or to everybody you might share something with. This said, I'm willing to bet it's time to squash some of the "very valid reasons" you think of for keeping your dream a secret.

For example, are you concerned about:

- *Looking stupid?*
- *Having a lack of professional experience and/or education in what you're interested in?*
- *Wanting to make sure everything is perfect before you get the word out?*
- *Worrying no one will care and failure will ensue?*
- *Feeling inadequate, scared, and intimidated to "put yourself out there"?*

Well, these two stories might help you think about this a little differently.

SHARING YOUR SIDE BUSINESS EARLY

Christina Hubbard is an account manager at a large ad agency in Los Angeles. She's always loved paper and had been toying with starting some sort of a side business around paper for more than a year.

I'd been encouraging her to tell people she's available to do custom gifts with paper (like cards) as a side business to start making it happen. But for quite some time, Christina felt many of the reasons I mention above and basically just "not ready."

However, soon after, she did try this advice. She put up *one* post on her Facebook and Instagram pages to tell people what she was up to and that she was now taking custom orders as a side business.

So what happened? This one post generated tremendous support and tons of comments. She had so much interest in custom projects that the greatest challenge she soon faced was time management to meet the demand! She experienced great momentum from that small step, but remember: Nothing actually changed about her story or what she can do for others. The only difference was that, with one announcement, people *knew* about it! Christina taking this step also inspired me to share her story with you, which is another win and opportunity for her young business.

Check her out at @christinahubbardstudio.

This is a great idea if you're starting a business, like Christina. This approach can also help you achieve personal or professional goals you have.

Here's another example, from me this time.

TELLING SOMEONE ABOUT
A PROFESSIONAL GOAL

As I mentioned in Chapter 2, when Gus and I were debating leaving LA and our jobs behind, one of the books that helped us make that decision was Richie Norton's *The Power of Starting Something Stupid*. I loved the book, its "The Bezos Test" exercise, and all the encouragement it gave us, so I decided to follow Richie online and sign up for his newsletter once we'd moved back to North Carolina.

More than a year later, in September 2014, Richie announced he was giving away free 45-minute strategy sessions. (He is a business coach in addition to being an author.) I signed up, jumping at the chance to talk to him directly and thank him for the impact his book had on our lives.

Though these sessions often tend to be a sales pitch, ours was a bit different. He had a program to sell, but we both realized through our conversation that I wasn't a great fit. Rather than just end the call, Richie really listened to me and asked about my goals for my business. I admired him so much that I decided to be pretty honest and voice some things I'd never said aloud before. I confessed that I was thinking more about more about becoming a professional speaker and teaching branding to other business owners, but I wasn't sure how best to get started.

Richie called my bluff and challenged me on the spot, having only just met me a half hour before. He said, "Okay, let's do it. Would you be interested in creating a pre-recorded 10-minute class for my new e-course?"

Um, yeah. Of course, I had no idea what the heck I was going to do for this, but I took Tina Fey's advice on the matter: say yes, and figure it out later. I couldn't believe this well-known author would offer me this kind of opportunity. And it was happening simply because I told him what I wanted to try.

Now, I just needed to make sure I didn't blow it. Sitting on the floor of my dad's bedroom, I recorded some voiceover, threw together my first slides in Keynote, and created my very first presentation for my business: "What's Your Story? 5 Ways to Strengthen Your Business Through Storytelling."

True to his offer over the phone, Richie included it in his Six Figure Platform course, where it's been available to all of his student entrepreneurs for the past four years. In that time, it's brought me three ideal branding clients and more than $10,000 in business. It was the basis and initial framework of a branding presentation that I've now given dozens of times across North Carolina after I began speaking live. And this opportunity is also part of what gave me the courage and ability to go after that big dream of public speaking just six months later (a story I share in Chapter 11).

None of this would have happened if I didn't tell somebody else what I was hoping to try next.

So what can you do? Whatever it is you are thinking about/dreaming about/considering as your next step, ask yourself: How many people *know* about these thoughts? Are there opportunities to tell more people? Whatever fear or hesitation I feel, am I overlooking and underestimating what doing this could mean for me?

Here's your opportunity to give it a shot right now.

TAKE ACTION EXERCISE

START TELLING PEOPLE ABOUT YOUR DREAMS RIGHT NOW!

HAVE HANDY: *Your computer or phone (any device with email)*

Send me an email at annie@anniefranceschi.com and tell me:
What is the next thing you want to try?

Maybe I don't know you but I've got the perfect thing or person to share with you if only I did. And even if I do know you personally, I may have no idea that you're interested in something I can connect you to. Maybe something you're working on could be a great collaboration for us. Or perhaps there's something personal you need to bounce off of someone and I could point you in a helpful direction. The point is that if I know, I can support you, keep an eye out for you—and maybe even put you to work like Richie did for me! And there are other people like me in your network, I'm willing to bet.

It all starts here, with a quick and simple email to annie@anniefranceschi.com.

Take the risk, face the challenge, and make sure at least one person knows what it is you're thinking about. I'm happy for that person to be me. *And hey, if this has you thinking or worrying about the risks of telling your friends and family ("What will people say?"), no worries: We get there in Chapter 9.*

CHAPTER 5

THE ONLY WAY TO CHANGE YOUR LIFE IS TO CHANGE IT

There's No Way Out but Through

Though we were working for the world's largest talent agency (Creative Artists Agency) and the world's greatest entertainment company (Disney), Gus and I knew we weren't happy with our lives and the direction our careers were going. In many ways, we were outward successes and inward messes when it came to our professional lives.

We'd spent months debating a crazy idea: moving back to my home state of North Carolina and starting over career-wise. We made our wheels-up, "yes" decision over burgers at In-N-Out on Washington Blvd. next to the Costco in Culver City. It would be another six months from that moment before we set foot back in North Carolina. I think about that meal a lot, not just because I miss In-N-Out—a lot.

I think about it because the reality is that no one was ever going to walk into that In-N-Out and say:

> *"Hey, are you Gus? Are you Annie? I've heard you're really unhappy in your careers so here are two plane tickets to North Carolina and two job offers awaiting you. Mazel tov! You've got this!"*

Life was not coming to offer us a way out—ever. No one was going to hand us plane tickets to North Carolina, or answers about what we wanted, or dream jobs, or dream lives.

This dinner was five years ago. We knew to some extent then, and I know for sure now: The only way to change our lives for the better was for us to change them ourselves. Change was only possible with action, with risks, with making something actually happen. After spending years at the mercy of unforgiving managers, praying for promotions, and dealing with corporate business politics, we finally chucked the waiting. We realized that we had to start being our own agents of change, because no one was going to do that for us.

We had to be the ones to sell our furniture.
To quit our dream jobs.
To buy our own plane tickets and fly 3,000 miles across the country.
To move in with my dad (which is really cool when you're 28 and married, by the way).
To find new jobs.
For me, to start a business.
For Gus, to identify physical therapy as the right career. And then, to spend three years investing himself—with choice after choice—in making that possibility a reality.

Actively changing big things in your life is like the truth you never want to face about diet and exercise. *"Doc, what can I do to lose weight? I'll do anything you tell me, except diet and exercise."*

After spending four years working tirelessly to earn a dream job at my favorite company on the planet, I decided over burgers to give it up so my life could change. I chose to make life possible and stop waiting for life to make things possible for me.

I've seen people I love and admire be stuck, for years—even decades—with the same complaints and frustrations. I've seen them live their lives at the mercy of where life leads them. They live in a reactive cycle that feels impossible to break. I know because I've lived in that cycle, too. When it comes to our life's happiness, I think we can all get caught up thinking that we're open to change—as long as it doesn't require "diet and exercise." We're open as long as it doesn't require us to make that change happen ourselves (and the risks we fear that come along with that).

So, will life decide for you or will you decide? *Because right now, the only way to change your life for the better is to change it yourself.*

Our very last In-N-Out as Californians in September 2013.
(Photo by Katie Morey)

Define Happiness and Success
for Yourself

It took me a while to realize that there isn't one shared definition of happiness.

For at least the first 20 years of my life, I thought there was just one shared collective idea of happiness that everybody subscribes to and that I needed to be chasing it. Maybe it was all the television I watched as an only child?

In any case, it took me what seems like forever to realize that, for most of my life, I had made decisions based on what I thought happiness was to "everybody," instead of defining what happiness was for me. That created a lot of internal conflict for me when my big career in the film industry didn't quite feel right. I was unsatisfied. I felt like I wasn't happy, though I was supposed to be. And it took a while and a lot of experiences to see that clearly.

Because I've been one of them myself, I think a lot of people are unhappy because they're subscribing to and focusing solely on the commonly held and "acceptable" societal definitions of happiness and success. While powerful, those definitions may or may not actually bring you happiness and success. We already know what it looks like; it's what I've called "the one path" throughout this book. So that being a thing, you need to realize that, in order to forge your own path, *you have to create your own definitions of happiness and success if you want to end up with a life you like.*

What exactly are happiness and success for you? Some people may aspire to be a huge executive at a major corporation. Others may want millions of dollars to make a movie or create a product. I thought something like that was what I wanted, but I slowly started to realize what would happen if one day, someone had handed me a bunch of money and said, *"Hey, Annie, go make a movie!"* I wasn't actually the least bit interested in doing that—when I stopped to think about it.

Why on earth was I on this path toward that? And why was I working so hard for it? It was because I thought I had to walk a certain direction to get to "career nirvana." I've since learned an important factoid: Career nirvana does not exist.

The first year that Gus and I were both living in Los Angeles, story development executive Maggie Malone took us to dinner. We first connected because Maggie is the daughter of a wonderful writing professor I had at Duke (Emmy Award–winner and novelist Michael Malone). She had generously agreed to show us the ropes since we were new to town. Bright-eyed and deep in the hustle, we soaked up every bit of advice Maggie had about how to make it in Hollywood. In our mid-20s, we were filled with optimism, faithfully walking the path—because, someday, it'd all be perfect, right?

I'll never forget what Maggie told us: We should realize, as we move up levels in our careers, that "the problems don't change. The walls just get sexier."

The problems don't change. The walls just get sexier.

There I was, imagining the development execs and producers had it on "easy street" and here was that sobering reminder: The problems aren't going to go anywhere. There is no point in your professional life when everything is perfect and when you won't be facing challenges. And I think when we don't know that, or remind ourselves of it, we end up chasing rainbows we'll never reach—simply because those rainbows don't exist.

I thought I had to stay in Los Angeles and have a big-deal job to be happy and successful. But I realized that I could choose what happiness and success were and make decisions accordingly. I could go somewhere like where I'm from (North Carolina), start a business, and create whole new definitions of happiness and success for myself—ones that proudly veered off "the one path."

To me, happiness means spending time with my husband and my family, and not spending my entire life commuting in the car. Success means empowering my clients, watching them grow, and making money to afford things like a house and a life (a lot easier to do when the cost of living is about half of what it is in LA). Joy means creating my own job title, instead of worrying when I'm going to get promoted. *(Side note: When you finally get to pick your own job title—CEO, founder, president, etc.—you realize that it's actually not that big of a deal.)*

Sometimes we have to reconsider and redefine what we are looking for in the first place. We need to stop and ask ourselves *why* before we continue to chase things we don't really want. Another person's view of happiness and success may be totally different from yours. That doesn't make theirs wrong. It doesn't make yours wrong, either, even if they or other people expect you to live by their definitions.

What's most important is that you take an active role in defining what happiness and success mean in your life and your career right now. Make decisions based on that, not on whatever societal notions of happiness and success may be hanging over you. Because the problems aren't going to change. The walls are just going to get sexier. Make sure you like the kinds of walls you're heading for.

| TAKE ACTION EXERCISE | CREATE YOUR OWN DEFINITIONS OF HAPPINESS AND SUCCESS |

HAVE HANDY: *Pen / pencil and two big sheets of paper*

1. Begin by getting out two big sheets of paper, the more monstrous the better. At the top of one, write "Happiness (noun):" and the other, "Success (noun):"

2. Start with whichever one you like. Look at the word, sit and think. Give yourself freedom to consider everything possible (a feeling, a dollar amount, a project, a person).

3. Then start writing bullet points. Get as specific as you can.

Here are some of my own examples, which may be helpful to you.

Happiness (noun):
- Having work/life balance
- Seeing movies in the theater
- Having Netflix nights with Gus
- Visiting Disney World
- Having fun, interesting, kind clients to work with
- Two words: Coke Icees!
- Playing Cards Against Humanity with friends
- Living in a beautiful house that feels like home
- Sunshine coming through my office window

Here, I'm defining happiness in both my personal and professional lives—because I want to be happy in both, right? I'm also noting small things, like Coke Icees and sunshine in my office, because I don't want to forget about those little things that can add joy to my life and make me feel happy. It's not just about the big things. All things of all sizes add up.

Here's what I'd put under my current "success" definition.

Success (noun):
- Making enough money with my business to save for retirement and put Gus through physical therapy school
- Sharing my story as a speaker in many different cities
- Helping my clients feel empowered as people and business owners
- Being respected and known for caring deeply about the success of my clients and collaborators
- Not feeling like I have to work all the time
- Being able to skip the alarm clock every day!
- Getting to have a flexible schedule of my own making
- Enjoying opportunities like podcast interviews, press, and other ways I get to meet new people, share my story, and help others
- Connecting with and becoming close with other entrepreneurs whose stories inspire me

I'm taking care to define what success looks like financially, and what business success is. It's even better if you write down actual dollar and number goals. It can be all too easy to constantly be seeking more success: more money, more clients, more notoriety. If I know what success is, and if I know it's not an infinite or impossible number to meet or status to reach, I can know when I have it. And I can appreciate that I have it.

Form your own definitions and put them somewhere you can see them every day. Encourage yourself to review them and revisit them as your life and career goals change. Just be sure to be using only these as your guidelines for happiness and success, so you can definitively know and fully enjoy those times that you have them at hand.

Make Space for the Life You Want

If you're coming along with me that it's important to define your own versions of happiness and success, I'd like to invite you to make some space for those things to be more possible.

If you want your life to change, ask yourself: *Am I making space for that to happen?*

As I've shared with you, no one was going to hand Gus and me airplane tickets and say, "Here you go. Here are your new, awesome lives in North Carolina!" We had to jump into uncertainty. We had to be willing to give things up. We had to be willing to sell our furniture and pack our things in exactly 73 UPS boxes. I had to be willing to give up a dream job, which I had spent years of tears and pain fighting to get. We had to do all of this to make space for possibility and for magic to happen.

If you want things to get better, you can't keep your life filled to the brim with things that hold you back. You have to make room for the opportunities that you want—even if you don't know what those are exactly. Whether it is packing a box or quitting a job, what can you do right now to make some space for things to happen?

It takes a lot of faith to change things, but you can always make a little more space. I had a friend during college who would text me for dating advice. He was always hung up on this one girl who wasn't a great fit for him. And I remember telling him that the longer he spent worrying and fixating on her, the longer he was taking himself off the market for somebody great.

The thing that I always wanted him to realize was that he wasn't leaving things open to possibility. He wasn't making himself available for the opportunity of a fantastic person who would value him. He was so stuck using his energies on the wrong girl, he wasn't making it possible for his dating life to change.

Look around and consider: Are you hung up on old things or ideas that are keeping new things from entering your life? What might happen if you let some of those things go? What if you break bad habits or finally quit the job that's weighing on you?

Sometimes making happiness and success possible can be as simple as clearing a landing strip for those things to happen in your life. Ask yourself: *Am I leaving margin?* Is there anything you can do to make more possibility and more space for something good or better to come in to your life?

Start now, because now is not the time to settle. Change a habit. Make some room. Create a bit more space for the life you want to materialize.

CHAPTER 6

DOUBT:
*"But maybe things aren't all
<u>that</u> bad . . ."*

PERMISSION:

YOU DESERVE MORE THAN "OKAY"

Life's Too Short
(to Keep Complaining
Over Coffee)

When I look back at my career in Corporate America, a lot of what I remember is being unhappy with my job and the corporate politics. I wasn't alone in that, as you might imagine. For example, as wonderful and fun a company like Disney is, it's still a corporation and there are politics in everything. And any organization is going to have politics, tough managers, and struggles to grow your career. My career was no exception.

So many times I bonded with my co-workers by going out to coffee or lunch and sharing our grievances. We were always trying to work out what our bosses were thinking. We were like the Sherlock Holmeses and Watsons of career development. We were trying to maneuver and figure out how we were going to get ourselves moving in our careers, despite all the challenges and difficult people we always faced. As if we were in a bad relationship, we would strategize and talk through things—over and over, and over again.

In hindsight, so many of those conversations were the same: the same arguments, the same troublesome people whom we just couldn't figure out, and, ultimately, the same complaints. We had spent so many years having what, in many ways, was the exact same conversation.

But why don't they value me?
Why don't they think I'm awesome?
Why won't they promote me?
Why won't they give me a chance to show them what I can really do?

I still don't know some of the answers to these questions across the various points and positions in my career. And as you know, I ended up quitting my job and starting my own business to work for myself, so I haven't had to worry about stuff like this for a while. But I digress.

It had been about two years since I had left my job and started Greatest Story when Gus and I returned to California for a friend's wedding. While I was in town, I had dozens of coffees with past co-workers and friends in the industry to catch up.

If there's one big thing I can tell you about that experience, it's that people were still having the same conversations. Some had moved from cubicles to offices or changed titles. Others had finally gotten some traction on things that we had talked about for quite some time. But there they were: the same problems with some of the same people—the same frustrations (though maybe some of the walls had gotten sexier). It wasn't everybody's story, but it was a story that was all too common. Oh, and given the state of the Los Angeles housing market, absolutely *nobody* wanted to know how much our townhouse in Durham, North Carolina, had cost.

I share this with you only to say that you don't want to settle or keep throwing "good time after bad." You don't want to spend years of your life complaining over coffee, having the exact same conversations with your co-workers. We all go through seasons like this in our lives, but you don't have to go through them forever—and if you're not careful, you will.

The only thing that's going to save you from this cycle is to see it clearly and take action to step out of it in some way soon. Years are going to go by and you will still be complaining about the same things. If you're not sure I'm right, do me a favor—tackle the next exercise.

| **TAKE ACTION** EXERCISE | **IDENTIFY AND SQUASH CYCLES OF NEGATIVITY** |

HAVE HANDY: *Pen / pencil and a portable notebook*

1. Start tracking the general subjects and situations that you talk about at work and in your personal life. As you start to identify them, you can create a hashtag for things like #stillnotpromoted, #stillnoraise, or #micromanagingboss.

2. Keep a tally by each theme, noting how many times you talk about it each day at work, home, or both.

3. Review and update it often.

You may be surprised at what active cycles you see in your life once you start keeping a record of all the times you shared the same challenges, fears, hopes, and dreams. The first step to breaking or changing a cycle is definitely to know and acknowledge one exists!

No Career or Business
Lasts Forever

Whether or not you're really frustrated with your professional life, it can be hard to imagine leaving it behind to do something new.

My dad's been a board member of a local non-profit concert organization in Fayetteville, North Carolina, for the past three decades. Beginning in 1991, he's helped to build it into a tremendous success and a well-loved hallmark of the community. And as much as he's loved being a part of that story and meeting legends like Tony Bennett and Michael Bolton, it's definitely required a tremendous amount of his time and resources. The hours he's put into it year after year for nearly 30 years could easily amount to an entire full career of their own.

Thinking to the future, my dad recently mentioned to a fellow board member that he was considering moving on to something new soon. She reacted with shock. She asked him in disbelief, "Michael, *you'd quit?*" He quipped in reply, "*Retire!* Not quit."

Why is quitting always a bad thing? Or retiring? Doesn't it have to be okay to move on sometimes, even from something you love or something you started? Being an entrepreneur, and the daughter and granddaughter of small business owners, something I'm learning is that businesses are a lot like people. They are born, they grow, and they have a life of their own in many ways. Careers can be this way too: They start, you grow with them, and they have good days and bad ones.

Like we *mere mortals*, careers and most small businesses will come to an end someday. They live and die as we do, so we can't give our lives over to them. And we cannot hang in there forever.

Whatever you're doing, if there's something bigger you want to try, but you're afraid to leave the business you started, or the job that needs you, remember that both things will be okay without you. The business may close. Your co-workers or boss might have a bit more work to do, but time will march on, and so will they.

A lot of people hang onto things because they are afraid of what will happen if they leave them behind: the program you created, the organization you rebuilt, and the co-workers who've been there for you through all the bad times. Will they be *okay?*

I'm reminded of what my co-worker Julie once said to me when I was worried about being out sick. It was an adage her mother had shared with her: *If you got hit by a bus, we'd figure something out.* A little morbid, but nonetheless true.

The obligations in your professional life will be there until you choose to walk away from them, you're let go, or your business really tanks beyond all hope. And you can't save your business, your job, or the company you work for from change and the unknown any more than you can do that for yourself.

You Can Give Up "Good" Things

Though no career or business lasts forever, it can be hard to leave things that are okay, or possibly even "good."

In many ways, the last position I had at Disney had become a dream job for the last six months I was there. The team restructured our responsibilities and had given me the oversight of managing the presentations for all of the titles we handled. Chapter 8 tells the story of how that transition happened. The short version is that it was actually a painful process that led to my job changing radically overnight. The switch and my new role gave me everything I'd been asking for for years. Getting what I'd always wanted also allowed me to see that this dream job wasn't ultimately going to make me happy. This is part of why I chose to give it up and move back to North Carolina to restart my career.

After I'd given my six-weeks' notice, I remember driving to Glendale for a meeting and talking to my dad during one of my last commutes. He said, "Are you sure you want to leave? Things sound like they're going really well!"

And he was right: They were going really well. In fact, they were going better than they ever had in my career to date. I'd been put in charge of managing a major part of a huge presentation for thousands of fans called D23. I was in meetings with senior-level executives who cared about my perspective. I was getting to work directly with filmmakers on how to tell their story through a presentation. Everything I'd been fighting for for years was finally at hand. *So should I walk away from success—especially when it was what I said I always wanted?* It was a fair question. And it was more than okay that my answer was *yes.*

Working at Disney's fan event, D23, in Anaheim, CA, in 2013.
(Photo by Gus Franceschi)

A term often used at big corporations and in the film industry is *golden handcuffs*. It's the notion of gaining so much success, fame, and fortune in a role that it'd be too hard to walk away from, even if your heart is pulling you in a new, exciting, but uncertain direction.

During my career at the studio, I started to wonder if I should leave to get a master's degree or an MBA. I asked the advice of my vice president boss, Jon. He'd had an impressive career in the film industry having worked for LucasFilm (*Star Wars*) before his time at Disney. I was very lucky that he hired me and spent several years taking me under his wing. He would often joke that I was his right hand or, as he'd call me to other executives, "Dotar No-jat" (a sarcastic spin on the phrase "Dotar Sojat" from an ill-fated film we'd worked on together, *John Carter*).

In that conversation, Jon encouraged me to think more broadly about my career and less about the next step or next degree. He pointed out that I needed to always be considering how I'd tell the story later to future employers. For example, would your make resume make sense if you explained why you went from one role, to another, or even to a master's degree program?

On this note, what I always remember about the conversation is this nugget of advice that Jon shared: When you make career moves, make sure you're running toward things, not away from them.

When you make career moves, make sure you're running toward things, not away from them.

I've learned that it takes courage to change your life, and it can be all that much harder when everything's going well. The key is to remember that change doesn't have to be about running away from something. It can be running toward something.

I was running toward a life that would make me fully happy so I didn't have to settle for what looked and sounded "good." There can be lots of good in your life and in your career, and you can still want to change things. It's okay to give up good to get great. If you're feeling pulled to move on—even if you are accomplished and have a job others would kill for—remember that it's *your* life, not theirs.

It's your story to write. What do you want to run toward?

DISCOVER HOW GOOD THINGS ARE
AND **WHAT GREAT LOOKS LIKE**

HAVE HANDY: *Pen / pencil and a sheet of paper or notebook*

1. If you're thinking of giving up something good or decently okay in your life or career, challenge yourself to make a list of the gaps you see in those things or the various ways that those things fall short of being what you fully want.

   For me, even though work was finally going well, I would have named these things on the day I had this conversation with my dad:

   - **Job Title:** I don't love my job title for the level of work I'm doing/people I'm working with. (I was an assistant manager and wanted to at least be a manager.)
   - **Pay:** I wish I could make significantly more money and have more control over that (rather than having to wait years for considerable raises).
   - **Office:** I don't have an office (just a noble cubicle with a lot of Muppet stuff).
   - **Work:** The work I do is fun and sexy, but it isn't changing lives. I wish I had more of a personal impact through my work and creative skills.
   - **Cost:** The cost of living in LA makes it hard to save for the future or to buy a house.
   - **Time:** We spend too much of our time commuting.
   - **Family:** I worry I won't be able to have much work/life balance if I have kids.

2. Now, look over your list and rank each one on a scale of 1–10 of importance to your happiness, with 1 being not very important and 10 being of the utmost importance.

Here's how I would have ranked that same list just as I was celebrating work getting "good" and being a "dream job":

- **Job Title—7**
- **Pay—10**
- **Office—8**
- **Work—10**
- **Cost—9**
- **Time—8**
- **Family—9**

3. After you've done your rankings, like I did above, how many 8s, 9s, and 10s do you see on your list? If you find there are many or that there are things that are really special to you that are at the high end of the spectrum, let these results nudge you not to settle for good or just okay!

   And know that, of course, no career is going to give you everything. The emphasis you put on your trade-offs will be different than mine. This is just a solid way to quantify your situation and do a true "gut check." Here's how the list would change if I did mine right now as a full-time entrepreneur in North Carolina:

   Vacation and Sick Days—3
   It'd be really nice if I could call in sick or get paid to go on vacation without having to plan for that. There are some days I wish I could just take off—but that's not in the cards when it's just me.

   Taxes—3
   It was so much easier when they came straight out of my paycheck! Dealing with taxes, receipts, and paying the full 15% for income tax instead of 7.5% (the other side split with an employer) is a doozy.

Missing Having a Work Family/Coworkers—2

I sometimes miss having buddies to go to lunch with at work and sharing the bond of being a work family. I'm grateful that I had five years of doing that and building those relationships, and I do get this kind of social time by having lunch dates with clients and collaborators, so I'd say the difference is a 2.

Employees/Team—4

I do have a stellar virtual assistant, but I don't currently have a team or any dedicated employees. I have no one to help me with the creative work. I'm not interested in what I'd need to do to change that right now, but there are weeks when I'm super-busy and wish there were more people to delegate to.

More Time for Passion Projects—4/5

I really love working on this book, but I have to do so on weekends and late nights while I prioritize client work and speaking. This probably goes hand in hand with hiring help. When this area gets to be a higher ranking, I'll have to deal with it and change course in some ways.

4. Now consider your list again before moving on. If you had significant 8s, 9s, or 10s right now, *guess what?* They just became your list of great goals to start running toward! Keep this list and use it as motivation to go get 'em, because now you know more specifically what you're looking for.

Fear the Status Quo

We've been talking a lot about the professional lives we already have—our status quo. When we have something "okay" to fall back on, it's the fear of change that holds a lot of power over us. Change freaks us out, right? At least we know how to deal with the problems in front of us. They are "the devils we know."

We know how to cope with the challenges that we already have.
What we don't know how to do is face the unknown.

What I want you to consider here is how scary it could be if nothing were to change. Imagine the status quo—the complaints, the fears, the problems, the things that terrify you day-to-day—continuing on for the foreseeable future: months, years, decades. How does that feel when you consider how long it could all go on for?

People often think the choice is to take a risk or not. Make a change, or just stay on safe where you are. But that's misleading. *You are taking a risk either way.* You are risking something whether you make a change or you surrender to the status quo. Both are active choices whether you're aware of it or not. If you choose one thing you're inherently not choosing something else.

I really like what comedian Jim Carrey has to say about this. In 2014, he gave a commencement speech at Maharishi University of Management. He talked about his father, Percy, who worked in "the safe job" as an accountant for the majority of his career. Though Percy was a gifted musician, he felt as though he had to get the paycheck to take care of his family and could not pursue that passion.

When Jim was 12, his dad was laid off from his accountant job. At age 51, Percy was left absolutely devastated after building a long and sensible career. Jim revealed in a 2011 interview for *Inside the Actor's Studio* that the entire family took on blue-collar jobs for years to recover financially. But in that graduation speech, Jim shares what he learned from watching his dad go through this: "You can fail at what you don't want, so you might as well take a chance on doing what you love."

We can't ignore the fact that if we don't choose change, we are actively choosing a life of status quo. And we should actually fear the status quo if it isn't making us happy. I went through this myself. I knew how to be successful "in the world of Hollywood" and I could make that work. It was scary and almost paralyzing to me to think about the unknown. I lived in the icky and safe-feeling status quo, clinging to it like a blanket for years.

For me, what ultimately happened is that I became more afraid of things *never* changing than of uncertainty and what might happen if they did. It's easy to forget, with how scary change can be, how freeing change can be as well. It can open us up to new adventures and make things better, not just worse.

Change is not always scary. Change is not always something to fear. But if you always come at it from a fearful perspective—if you assume that you'll always be safe and happy to choose the road you already know *(with its thorns along the way)*—you may be short-changing yourself.

CHAPTER 7

DOUBT:
"Maybe in a year or two.
Now is not the right time."

PERMISSION:

THE BEST TIME IS ALWAYS NOW

It's Never Easier Later

According to my dad, my grandfather Herbert always used to say, "The more sh*t you have, the more problems you'll have." This quote has been coming to mind often, especially as I get older and have to worry about things like insurance and what's going on in the political spectrum.

I find myself thinking of this when I'm at a crossroads. I'm reminded that it's never going to be easier to make a really hard decision. Obviously there are going to be exceptions to everything. (For example, you may be super-close to graduating from professional school or paying off a large debt.) But in terms of the things that weigh on you that make you worried that you can't do it—that you can't be successful at whatever you want your next chapter to be— that decision is never, ever going to be an easier one to make than it is *right now.*

Life is always going to get more complicated. There will always be more expenses. There will always be more responsibilities. There will always be more excuses why you can't do the thing that scares you, yet is the thing that you really want to do. It can be helpful to recognize that it's not ever going to be easier to face that reality.

If you're not sure this is true, just remember how much simpler your life seemed a decade ago, or even five years ago. I was at my 10-year college reunion recently with my girlfriends from my freshman-year dorm. We were talking about what a doozy our 30s have been so far compared to our 20s! That said, I'm willing to bet we'll be back on campus in our 40s wishing for the rose-colored glasses that our 30s "had been."

The nature of life is that you're never going to find yourself with a free week or a free month with just absolutely nothing to do but jump into a new life or career. When's the last time you even had a free *day* out of nowhere on your calendar? That's not how this works at any stage, except maybe retirement. And by then, the question is: Will you have done the things in your professional life that you really wanted to do?

We can't keep waiting for another day when things will become simpler and less complex. The nature of life is complication. I regularly talk to my dad on the phone, and he's fond of saying that he's got "a million things to do" that day. I try to remind him that there are always going to be problems to solve. That's sort of what life really is: a never-ending series of facing problems and solving them, with the occasional Netflix binge. He's never going to find a time to catch his breath if he's focused on waiting for all those problems to clear his deck. It just won't happen. There's always too much to do and not enough time to do it.

My last day in Corporate America was September 4, 2013. Like most people, to help me stay organized, I'd kept a running list by my desk that I would update from time to time. And of course, I had a couple of projects outstanding on my list that day.

Do you know what happened on September 4, 2013? Those last tasks went unchecked. I didn't finish any of them. *(I'm sorry to the team about that one. My bad!)* But the reality is just like this: We're never going to get through our to-do lists—in our careers and in our personal lives.

We're never going to satisfy all the responsibilities, commitments, and things that we have signed up to do. We can't wait for our plates to be clear, for us to not be solving a million problems, and for there to be nothing else on our minds besides our dreams.

We have to make the space for them. And it's time that we get moving, because life is already in motion.

On the lot on my last day, September 4, 2013.
(Photo by the author)

Life Will Surprise You

My friend Trish Gonnella Russo was just like me. Actually, she wasn't just like me. She was a few more years into her career in the film industry than I was when we met. I looked up to her and her second-in-command, Jessica. At the time, Trish was the assistant to the president of production at Disney. She was working her way to become a development executive or a production executive. Trish was basically on "the one path" that I wanted to be on. And she is warm, funny, and a good, encouraging friend.

We had lunch together when schedules would allow it. During one lunch, at Joy Feast, the Chinese place just down the street from the lot, we were talking about the holidays and our upcoming family celebrations.

A few weeks later, in January, I stopped by Trish and Jess's office to drop off documents for their boss. I noticed that Trish's hair looked different, so I mentioned it. *"Oh, your hair looks great. Did you get it cut?"*

She looked at me and said, *"No. Actually I was diagnosed with cancer and this is a wig."*

Just like that, Trish's story had changed. Even my relationship to her had changed. I had such egg on my face, right? *Ugh.* What a terrible thing I had just said. Trish was maybe two or three years older than I was at the time, and had turned 30 six months prior. She had her whole life ahead of her, and there she was telling me, after we had hung out just a few weeks earlier, that she'd been diagnosed with cancer and was going through chemotherapy.

It's hard to believe that that was nearly seven years ago. Trish's whole life story had completely changed in those weeks between our lunch and when I saw her in the office. In the time that has passed since, Trish has battled cancer and gone into remission. She has become an incredible advocate for stage IV breast cancer, metastatic breast cancer, and cancer in general. But this wasn't Trish's original life plan. She was going to be this incredible producer; she wasn't going to be the person with cancer, or the young person with cancer, or—what her story really has brought to light—the person who wanted to be a mother but couldn't (traditionally) due to cancer.

Trish's life story got rewritten by what happened to her. But then, she chose to rewrite her own story. She could have let her hopes and dreams fall apart but instead, she changed with the change in her life and rose to the challenges at her feet. She's raised thousands for metastatic breast cancer research over the years and her latest achievement is having created a documentary with her husband about overcoming their infertility after cancer through surrogacy. *Love Always, Mom* premiered in 2018 at the Bentonville Film Festival. It won the "Audience Award," which Trish got to celebrate with her husband, Greg, and their young son, Grayson, in attendance.

Trish has really inspired me. I used to think about her a lot. I admit it was often because her story scared me. I would wonder, *What would happen to me if I got sick at such a young age?* And the other thing it makes me think about is how suddenly life can and most likely will change your story.

We haven't been immune to this kind of life twist either. On November 10, 2015, Gus's story changed. It was the day before his two-year anniversary at his marketing job here in North Carolina,

The official poster for Trish's documentary, Love Always, Mom. *Follow the film using @lovealwaysmomthemovie on Instagram, Facebook, and other platforms.*
(Photo by Mel Stone Photo, courtesy of Cyan Gray Hope Foundation)

...ce on which he was scheduled to receive an anniversary annual raise of $5,000. We were excited, and I was spending the morning entertaining a crazy idea: What if we moved some money around and made a run at paying off our home mortgage?

To explain more fully why I had this hair-brained notion at only age 30, we are big Dave Ramsey nerds. If you don't already know Dave, he's the author of *The Total Money Makeover* and *Financial Peace*. Gus and I discovered his books and podcast/radio show ("The Dave Ramsey Show") in our first year of marriage. I wish I'd always known about him because he's taught us not just to save, but *how* to save and how to stay out of debt. Thanks to Dave Ramsey, we were able to save thousands before we left LA, leave LA in the black, buy a car in cash, and put down 20% on our house when we bought it. So on that morning in November I was anxious to move ahead in Dave's "7 Baby Steps" to wealth and jump to step 6: pay off your home mortgage early.

While running the numbers, knee-deep in Excel, I received a phone call that killed the debt-free party and my optimistic outlook. Gus had been brought into his boss's office and let go. The team overall wasn't doing well sales-wise, and it seemed he was cut to avoid having to give him that anniversary raise the next day.

Just like that, I was the breadwinner for the first time since becoming an entrepreneur, Gus was scrambling to find a new job, and we were worried about our future instead of filled with excitement. So began a six-month adventure in uncertainty, as my clients dried up for the first time in the history of my business and Gus struggled to find a new role with setbacks and another layoff along the way. It was one of the toughest, most desert-like seasons we'd ever gone through.

Life was showing us that our perfect plans could change on a dime without our input.

Life happened to us yet again a year later when we were officially diagnosed with infertility in August 2016. At that moment, my story changed. Life said, "Hey, Annie. Infertility is going to be part of your journey." Just like Trish's life said, "Hey, Trish! Cancer is going to be part of your story," and Gus's life said, "Hey, Gus. A new job and path are going to be part of your story, whether you like it or not."

These are things that none of us chose to experience, but we experienced (and continue to experience) them nonetheless. I'm learning that not only will life change your story, it's really about *what you do* when that happens.

You can't assume that you're never going to have things like this happen to you. Sometimes people get diagnosed with cancer—even young people who are amazing, like Trish. Sometimes the safe and stable job you're counting on gets pulled out from under you or you're not going to have an easy path to having children, though it can seem like everyone else does.

Things will become a part of your life overnight. I never thought that infertility would be a part of my story, but it is now a very significant part of my story. It's one that doesn't have an ending quite yet—and may not, to be honest. What matters is what I do now that my story has changed.

Trish didn't give up. She reinvented her life. She fought like a warrior, and she continues to fight. She has become defined by her challenges and her struggles, and she is always rising to the occasion and finding ways to tell stories, realize a career, and be the mom she's always wanted to be.

I try to take Trish as an example for the things that I struggle with in my life that have unexpectedly become a part of my story. More people than you realize care about what you do and are moved by it. We are all going through tough things, whether we share them publicly or not.

If there is one truth about life, it's that it will change. And it doesn't always have to be something like cancer that can change life for us. What matters is how we change and how we embrace those twists and turns in our story. What makes a difference is when we choose to turn them into something beautiful instead of something that pulls us down into the weeds.

You can be an agent of change. I never thought that I would have my own business or become an entrepreneur. I chose that life for a number of reasons. One was because I didn't want to work for someone else anymore. Another was that I wanted to be creative with my skills. And I took action to change my life, and that story has changed with it, with me being involved.

Life will suddenly change around you. It's something that is going to happen in some way, maybe in multiple ways, to so many of us. What are you going to do now, if you choose not to wait for one of life's unexpected turns?

Consider What Your Legacy Will Be

Have you ever considered whether the work you do now will live on? Whether you work for yourself, or work for someone else, the question is the same.

Are you doing something with your life that will leave a mark? *That will inspire stories between people you may never meet? That will continue to change lives long after you do it?*

I could ask you, "What will your legacy be?" But I think we all look at that question and feel daunted, maybe even disconnected. Who am I to have a legacy? I'm not some kind of nobility or a super-important person. But the thing is, we will all leave behind stories.

I think about my mother, Barbara Jean Saunders. She was a fiercely passionate, caring mom and justice seeker. She was also a small business owner who sold wedding invitations and did calligraphy under the name You're Invited. I was lucky to have her with me for the first 17 years of my life, until she passed away unexpectedly in 2003 from a pulmonary embolism.

Talk about life rewriting your story. I lost her when I was a teenager. She'd never know where I went to college, or meet my husband, or be able to help me figure out this adult thing. Everything just stopped, cold, on April 16, 2003. But did the memories have to stop? This is what I started wondering six years ago. Just because she isn't here with me, why do the stories and the memories have to end? What if I started to celebrate her and make new memories?

This led me to create a holiday around her birthday, which I call

Barbara Day. Since 2012, I've hosted Barbara Day every August 17th. It's a celebration of her life and an open invitation to anyone who knew her to remember her, talk about her, share stories, and do something in her honor. Hosting this has led to so many wonderful experiences and, in many ways, new memories of her for me and for the people who loved her too. Across the Barbara Days and in the years that have followed, I have been humbled by the legacy she never knew.

Legacy is a fancy word for impact. Legacy is the ways in which the things you do now, what you create, what you share with others, and how you help others will go on to affect more lives—far beyond your original intent. I feel like what I've learned about legacy, I've learned from the experiences that have happened to me after my mother died.

Across the years, so many people have told me stories about her and how the things she did for them stuck with them. *Your mom did my wedding invitations. Your mom did all of my daughter's calligraphy! Everyone loved it! It was so special!*

Years ago, when Greatest Story offered wedding branding services, I got an inquiry from Catherine, a bride I went to high school with. She included this story along with her email to me:

> *"My parents have a wall in their house devoted to wedding portraits of all of the members of my family tree, branching out from my parents all the way to my great-great-grandparents.*
>
> *My two brothers and their wives are up there too, and I'll be up there soon! Underneath every portrait are the names of the couple*

*and the date of their marriage, written in beautiful calligraphy, by
your mother, I believe!*

*. . . I thought you'd like to hear that her writing is still proudly
displayed in our living room!"*

My mom isn't here, but she's a part of Catherine's family history. I
had no idea about this picture wall until I heard this story, but I'm
told a memory just like it every few months. My mother may never
have imagined all the stories that keep reaching me, in the months
and years after her passing.

I don't think my mother thought her work would live on the way it
has. But I think her story is so resonant because it's not necessarily
"special." My mom wasn't famous. She was a small business owner
and someone who liked to help people by creating beautiful things.
People threw away thousands of envelopes with her calligraphy on
them, just as we throw out wedding envelopes we get in the mail. But
the work she did, the care she put into it, the very genuine intention
behind it all, somehow—even across time—sticks with people. It
lives on.

My mom didn't have to have a fancy job title, or super-important
clients, or make a ton of money. Nevertheless, she left a legacy. I've
seen it firsthand so many times over the past 15 years. She had a
bigger impact on far more lives than she would have ever considered.
I'm continually amazed as her daughter to learn new stories as the
years go by.

That's the thing about the work you do, the family you create, and
the ways you spend your time. You get up every day and you invest

Don't Quit

When things go wrong, as they sometimes will,
When the road you're trudging seems all uphill,
When the funds are low and debts are high;
And you want to smile, but you have to sigh;
When care is pressing you down a bit,
Rest if you must, but don't you quit.
Life is queer with its twists and turns
As every one of us sometimes learns,
And many a fellow turns about
When he might have won had he stuck it out.
Don't give up though the pace seems slow,
You may succeed with another blow.
Often the goal is nearer than
It seems to a faint and faltering man;
Often the struggler has given up
When he might have captured the victor's cup;
And he learned too late when the night came down,
How close he came to the golden crown.
Success is failure turned inside out.
The silver tint of the clouds of doubt,
And you never can tell how close you are;
It may near when it seems afar;
So stick to the fight when hardest hit,
It's when things seem worse that you mustn't quit.

A poem my mother hand-lettered—It was mailed back to me by some of her friends in Pennsylvania. She had created the print to encourage them during a difficult season, and they thought I'd appreciate having it.

yourself in something. You invest yourself in someone. I want you to know for a fact: It creates ripples. It does matter. So, *do it on purpose.*

The small projects you create, the products you sell, the meetings you run—I promise that you have no idea how they will echo across others' lives and future generations. We aren't aware of this in our daily lives. We tend to feel insignificant or that we haven't done enough yet to have a legacy one day. We feel like we aren't creating meaning. But if you're committing your passion to your purpose (through a business, your job, volunteer work, or taking small steps to a new dream), you are already building legacy.

I guarantee you that more people read what you write than you will ever know. (Trust me: It shocks me all the time that it's not just my dad and husband who read my newsletter and blog.) More people are inspired and taking action because of you than you realize. There will be many more stories and ways in which you will have shaped people's lives. Some you will hear, and some you won't, but know that is the nature of doing good work in the world.

I encourage you to run your business, plan your career, or choose your volunteer opportunities with this kind of attention. Live your life like you are building a legacy, because the truth is, you are. If you go forward with this in mind, maybe you'll make different decisions—better decisions—within your business or career, and by doing so, change even more lives.

I appreciate my mom and the lessons she's taught and continues to teach me, even in the years that she hasn't been here. Because of her, I've seen why legacy is possible for all of us. For me, following in her footsteps, I know legacy is critical to what I do, as I continue her story and start telling new ones. That's exactly why my business name, Greatest Story Creative, came from tremendous purpose and intention. It is about reminding us all (me included) that life is truly the greatest story you get so you have to live it well—knowing you can and will impact other lives.

Know you're building a legacy and that what you do has so much more impact that you realize. *The time is now to plant the seeds.*

**DREAM AND DEFINE
YOUR IDEAL LEGACY**

HAVE HANDY: *Pen / pencil and a sheet of paper or notebook*

No matter what life or career move you make next, be sure of this: You're going to leave some kind of legacy.

Right now is your opportunity to dream and define what you'd like it to be, so let's do it.

- Brainstorm this question: **What would your ideal legacy be?** Whether professional, personal, or both, here are some questions to get you started.

  Imagine historians did a report on your life. How would you like to see these questions answered?

  - *What would I want people to say about my work to others?*
  - *What would I want others to do with my work? Keep it in their homes? Use it in other ways? How? Be specific.*
  - *What would I want people to remember about my career?*
  - *What would I want people to say about me to others?*

- *How would they say I made them feel? And treated them?*
- *What would be other peoples' favorite things about me?*
- *What would I be best known for?*
- *What qualities and stories would my friends remember most about me?*
- *What qualities and stories would my family remember most about me?*

Feel free to answer as if you've accomplished things even if you haven't tackled them yet. The key is that your answers don't have to be accurate right now—just possible that you could make them come true later in your life and career.

Even if you tackle just a few of these at a time, what you're doing is continuing to craft a measurable road map for your future. A list like this is a powerful vision of your *whys* and the story you want your life and career to ultimately write.

Between this exercise and the others throughout the book, hopefully you're beginning to see that you have lots of opportunities to build upon your already-existing legacy.

Face Your Feelings, Failures, and Fears

CHAPTER 8

DOUBT:
*"But I'm afraid to face
how I really feel."*

PERMISSION:

THE TRUTH
WILL SET YOU
FREE

Tell Other People the Truth

I've told you about how I quit my dream job. What I haven't told you yet is that just before I was moved into that job, I was uncomfortably close to getting fired, and it brought me to a turning point that would define my film industry career.

It's a story of how you can be feeling so near failure, how a pivot can change your life, and why you need to tell other people the truth you feel—even when it's ugly and you're terrified of what they'll say.

So what led me to almost getting fired? Through organizational shifts on our team, I ended up with the least "high-profile" movies (basically, the direct-to-video leftovers). While I was grateful to find potential in the less-exciting projects, it put me in a bit of a catch-22 situation. There wasn't a lot to do on those projects, and when I did try to move things forward, I was met with resistance (since they weren't priorities).

I was struggling to show what I was capable of with what was on my plate and frustrated that I had little to do. One day my manager, Dominique, asked me into her office. She told me that Leslie, the head of our department, was concerned that I wasn't working on "anything."

What do you mean, not working on anything? This felt like a gut punch. My hands had been tied and now—somehow—my job was on the line because of it?

What was I supposed to be doing without much at all to work on?

Confused and upset, I chose to confess to my boss what I'd really been feeling for years. I said the thing you're afraid to say, even though it's true, because you're going to look unprofessional.

I said, definitively but while quietly fighting back tears, *"It's like you guys love me, but you have no idea what to do with me."* It was the unvarnished, uncomfortable truth. It also changed everything.

Dominique heard me when I shared that I felt stuck—with my hands tied and like I wasn't being given the work that really showed what I could do. She came in the next day with a recommendation that changed the trajectory of my career and my life. She and Leslie restructured my role to cover *all* of the upcoming movies, but as the communications lead. This way, I could play to my strengths on a full-time basis, by writing and designing story presentations. I'd have plenty to do and a lot to contribute.

It was a new idea. It was a pivot. It made everyone's lives easier and it paid off that very afternoon. With that change, I went from my job on the chopping block to being our department's go-to, well-loved communications person basically overnight. Is this normal? I don't know. What I do know is that from the moment the idea was pitched, that same day I was meeting with Leslie and helping her with presentations for major studio leadership. The new and unexpected arrangement fit us all—me especially—like a glove.

I didn't get fired after all. In fact, I got to enjoy a six-month ride in a job that was created to play to my strengths, doing some of the most exciting work I would ever do during my time there. Getting to live up to and show off my potential was a gift and a blessing to me in many ways. As I've shared throughout this book, it even showed me that my dream job was not going to give me a dream life.

When I ultimately chose to quit this new dream job months later, it was for all the right reasons. I wasn't running away or being let go for being misunderstood. I left on good terms with everyone—in particular Leslie, who I had been terrified was going to fire me not too long before. I still get choked up thinking about my last day in the office when she ran after me to catch me at the elevator for one last hug. It was an amazing moment with a person whom I thought I was terribly disappointing not so long before. It was lasting proof to me that so much can change when you are honest about your feelings.

To this day, I remain immensely grateful for that, because there were so many moments when I thought that if I left, it would be about quitting and giving up. Instead, it was about running toward a new life and feeling bittersweet about letting the newly found, good one go. I left my dream job on a high note, with relationships I still treasure and lessons that taught me about not giving up, managing relationships, figuring out how to work with people who have different styles from you, and finding your place. I have Dominique to thank for that, and I have myself to thank—if only for being brave enough to speak the words I thought would make me look weak and unprofessional.

This experience taught me a lot about failure, success, and all that's in-between. I share this story of vulnerability with you to illustrate the point that you can be this close to failing, to getting fired, to falling flat on your face—and then things can change. Something as simple as being honest with the people in your life can make that happen.

I also share it with you because of this quote from Albert Einstein:

> *"Everybody is a genius.*
> *But if you judge a fish by its ability to climb a tree,*
> *it will live its whole life believing that it is stupid."*

For so many years, I was the fish, being told I had to climb the tree. It got to me on so many car rides home in LA traffic, where I would bawl my eyes out. I felt really stupid. I felt really lost. The reality was, I just wasn't in the right role. I needed that pivot. I needed a change of perspective.

In your season, what small change could make a big difference? *Who* can you tell how you are really feeling?

Whether you work for yourself or for someone else, in the places where you struggle, what's one small change you could make? What's one outside-the-box shift you could consider? A little pivot can do a whole lot of good.

And if you're feeling like that fish being asked to climb trees all day, just know there's a better direction for you—one you can make happen. You know it to be true, deep down.

Be Honest with Yourself

Sometimes, life punches you in the face. And sometimes, you actually need it to.

This was what happened to me after I left Los Angeles and Gus and I moved back to North Carolina in fall 2013. I had taken a huge leap of faith to quit and move back home to North Carolina to figure out my purpose and explore big dreams. But then I began job searching for a full-time job with benefits, hoping to do that as a safety net and start Greatest Story Creative as a side business first.

Why did I do this? Well, because looking for jobs was the smart, societally right thing to do while I figured out a real "plan." It was a version of "the one path" that of course, I'd need to ultimately walk to become a successful entrepreneur (you know, start a side hustle, build up savings, go full-time, etc.). *Ugh.* In hindsight, it seems like I hadn't learned anything from taking a big risk, changing my life, and moving 3,000 miles. There I was, on the heels of having jumped farther than ever, about to go hide, all nice and cozy, in a comfortable job with benefits.

At the time, little did I know, the truth was in plain sight, even if I was afraid to look it square in the eyes.

In months of this job searching process, I'd befriended the president of a local advertising agency. She was impressed with my Hollywood experience. After hiring me for a consulting project or two, she started working on creating a full-time job for me at the agency. During the process, I came into the office for a "touch base" meeting with her, but I ended up in a meeting with the president's number-two executive instead. I'll call her Sandra.

I thought I'd been asked to come in for an informal chat to nail down job details. However, I quickly realized that I was suddenly in the middle of an intense job interview. *Crap—worst feeling of being unprepared ever!*

On the spot, Sandra asked me why I wanted to work in marketing and advertising. I answered her honestly and positively:

> *"Because I want to work on local brands and help them make a difference."*

Upon hearing this, she started *laughing in my face.* Chuckling. Guffawing.

She barely got out the following reply:

> *"You want to make a difference . . . in marketing?!"*
> *(Subtext: "What an idiot!")*

Have you ever had someone actually laugh in your face? We all say people do this, but to have it actually happen to me was a bit nuts. A hearty laugh at my dream and passion! That sucked. Nevertheless, I think about this story fairly often, even years later. And I'll tell you: I'm mostly compelled to send this woman a fruit basket, because I owe a lot to this moment in my life.

After this confrontation, I was forced to finally face the truth of how I was really feeling. I got out of that meeting politely, then spent the next 45 minutes driving home and bawling my eyes out to my dad. I told him the real, deep-down truth. I knew exactly what I wanted to do for a job: I wanted to run Greatest Story full-time. The reason

I wasn't doing that and was pursuing other jobs was mostly because I was scared out of my mind to try it.

I finally spoke the truth I was afraid to speak—for fear I'd actually have to face it. I didn't really want to work for anyone else. I was just terrified I'd fail if I went out on my own. I wanted to take the "easy route." But Sandra's reaction forced me to see that the easy route was copping out. She didn't buy it, and that particular job wasn't how I really wanted to make a difference. She was the mirror I needed—maybe not the one I wanted, but the one I needed, at the right time.

I began debating what the heck I was going to do. The fear I felt was very real. At the time, Gus and I were living with friends and didn't have an apartment of our own. I was worried I wouldn't make enough money and that I'd embarrass myself if I really tried this entrepreneurship thing for real.

Friends tried to talk me out of it. They advised me to do Greatest Story part-time and the other job at the same time. But as I was now being brutally honest with myself, I was realizing there was no in-between if I was going to give something my all. I don't know how to do my "Annie" thing at 25% or 50%. I only know how to be 100% me at something. I'd just had a five-year career out of college at that point that I'd given 100% of me to and then been left trying to make do with whatever potential remained after hours and on the weekends. And what was I getting ready to do? Do it all over again.

I was going to trade an opportunity to see what I really could do if I gave myself a chance for the "job security" of an ad agency job, working for somebody who literally laughed in my face. After conversation after conversation with friends, family, Gus, I could see it: *They* weren't the people I needed to convince that it was okay to go full-time. That person was me.

I decided to make a bargain with myself. I told Gus that I'd give myself permission by giving myself one year to try full-time and in the meantime we'd budget to live almost entirely on Gus's slightly better-than-entry-level salary. This allowed me to feel not totally irresponsible for following my hunch of a dream. If I bombed, I'd go looking for a job in 12 months. It's what I had to do to finally tell myself it was okay to go full "Annie" and answer the question clearly, once and for all: Can I be a successful as a business owner?

Then came the part where I had to tell the president of the agency, a woman who'd at that point spent weeks putting together a job for me, that I didn't actually want it. *Awkward.* I was so nervous to get on the phone with her, and I felt terrible for wasting her time. There was also part of me that was worried I was making a mistake.

Nevertheless, I sucked in my breath, dialed her number, and faced my big fear. I thanked her; then I said that I had chosen to take my business full-time. I explained that I couldn't live always wondering what might have happened if I had just given myself the chance to try this—to do what both scared and fascinated me.

Moments into me lowering the boom of turning down the job, she replied, *"Well, do you still want to work on things with us?"*

Um, yep.

"Great, we'll call you later today with the details to get started on a new project."

And just like that, within minutes of turning away from what was "safe" and choosing to go full-time, I'd booked my next Greatest Story client.

I'd given myself a year from that moment to build a sustainable business as a full-time entrepreneur. It's been more than four years since then, and I still pinch myself when I think about how I've never had to stop and look for a full-time job. The business has grown considerably every year and, over time, I've been able to make significantly more money on my own than I was making when I left the film industry. I've had more than 150 clients and been a part of telling so many stories of incredible people. I got to answer the question and finally see what I was capable of, and it was solely because I took the leap and chose to hire myself.

If you're feeling like *Hang on. Hey, it was easy for you to do this. You had a spouse's salary that made it possible,* I totally get it. You should know that there were many times that I've wondered: Should I even be writing this book? Should I share my stories? Maybe what I've gone through hasn't been hard *enough* or tough *enough*. I often worried that my perspective wasn't valuable because there are so many more impressive, inspiring stories of people who greatly defy the odds of their careers and circumstances and find success.

And it's absolutely true that I am and was blessed to have a husband who had a salary that, with a tight budget, we could rely on while I started my business. I was also lucky to have a dad I could move in with for free when I gave up my Hollywood career, and that he provided for my Duke education. These are all things that I'm tremendously grateful for, and I realize that not everyone has the same opportunities when they're considering changing lives or careers. But for your own sake, I ask you to be careful not to let the excuses of someone else having this or that opportunity keep you from carving out the life you want—even if that someone is me.

I've chosen to share my story here, despite worrying it's not good enough or helpful enough, because maybe it will help you or someone else. I realized that it was okay to give myself permission to share this with you for this simple truth: There will always be people who've had it harder than I have, and there will always be people who have had it easier. That's true for me, and it's also true for you.

No matter the path I've led and shared with you here in this book, your story has always been destined to be different. So it's not "Do exactly what I did" as much as me wanting you to know that you're not alone in the struggle and the possibility of reinventing yourself. I hope you find the inspiration here to apply these ideas to your own life and the courage to do what you can with what you have, even and especially when it means taking smart risks on the things that matter most to you.

For me, January 25, 2014, was the day I took one of my biggest risks, made that fateful call to turn down the job, and officially went full-time in my business. It's one of my favorite dates now because it was the day I was honest with myself and that truth set me free.

Wherever you are in your journey, what's on your heart? What do you know to be true about what you want? And *when* (what date) will you own it?

MAKE A DATE
WITH YOUR OWN DESTINY

HAVE HANDY: *A red pen + calendar or an online calendar*

- Think of something you've been putting off, big or small; or it could be something deep down you've been afraid to face. Got it?

- Now just do one simple thing. Take a red pen and circle the first date in the future that you see on your calendar. (If you're more digital, do this with an online calendar by setting a calendar reminder.)

- However you note it: On that day, this month, this year, it's time to do the thing. Face the scary and pick up the phone to quit the job, or send the email, or make that change you've been putting off. You and I both know that it's time to do it. I mean, it's scheduled right there in your calendar.

CHAPTER 9

"But what will other people say?"

PERMISSION:

PEOPLE WILL SURPRISE YOU. LET THEM.

You'll Get More Support
Than You Think

For years, one of the biggest things that kept me from changing my path and direction was worrying what other people would say.

I was so terrified that others would judge me for quitting and changing my plans. I worried what others would think of me if I gave up on the things I'd always said I wanted. I wondered if people would think I was crazy and that I'd disappoint my friends, family, and team.

But the lessons I learned by telling people were two fold:

> *People will surprise you.*
> *You should let them.*

Here's why. In March 2013, after I'd put off what was right in my heart for many years, I had finally made the decision to leave the film industry altogether (I share in Chapter 5 that this happened over burgers at In-N-Out.) A few months later, in July 2013, I faced one of my greatest fears of doing that: telling everyone at work. For so long, I had put off this decision, worrying that I was ruining my career and that people would judge me. I was fairly sure that many, especially those with major success at the company, would think I was nuts and discourage me for giving everything up—especially without having a job or a big plan already lined up.

Then came the time to bite the bullet. I stayed after a meeting to talk to the head of our department, Leslie. I asked if we could talk for a minute. She asked, "Sure, do you and Gus have some family updates?" excitedly assuming I might be pregnant.

Eek. That's where I leveled the boom. I told her that I was going to give up the dream job they'd created for me just months before, and that I was going to leave—now that things were great—to go back to North Carolina and figure out a new game plan. I let all this roll out, all the while afraid I was massively disappointing her.

Without missing a beat, Leslie said, "Annie, I know you're going to be very successful, but that success doesn't necessarily have to be here at Disney."

She wished me well and was sad to see me leave, as were my boss, Dominique, and my incredible team/first true work family. But maybe this was just because they had been there with me in the trenches for nearly four years. What would everyone else say?

In the weeks following, I asked my friends across the company to coffee before I left. I met with every level of employee at the studio, from interns and assistants, to senior and executive vice presidents. I was sure that I'd hear "You're crazy" from plenty of them. But people surprised me.

I got one of two reactions, across dozens of conversations:

> *"Congratulations! I am so thrilled for you and can't wait to see what you do."*

> *"I'm so jealous. I wish I could leave and do something totally different!"*

Jealous? It was the second reaction that really stunned me, especially as I heard it from people who'd been at the company for five years, 10 years, even 20+ years. *They were jealous of me? Why?* Well, as it turned out, I learned that we all have these crazy thoughts in the back of our minds about changing our lives. I discovered in these moments that it is rare and it is powerful to act on them.

Would I have acted sooner on changing my career path had I known how people would react and how supportive they would be? I think so. My hope is that in sharing this, you'll consider what people might say and realize it may not be discouraging. (And if this is something you're worried about, I'm getting to that next.)

What would happen if other people in your life actually "got it"? What if you discovered that they'd totally be in your court about trying something new and changing your life? What if they secretly felt the same way you do?

You'll never know unless you tell them.

My team gifted me this "Annie" drawing by Disney artist Christopher Shin as a goodbye gift. It's now on display in my home office.

When Family and Friends Discourage You, It's Not about You

Surprise cuts both ways. When you want to try something new, not everyone will surprise you with a great reaction. I've had a couple of my closest friends discourage me from taking risks and doing the things I've been most passionate about. But here's why I'm grateful for that.

When we returned to North Carolina in 2013, I found myself at a new crossroads, torn between taking a job that was being created for me at a local ad agency or going full-time with my branding business. As I shared in Chapter 8, after many tears and a confrontational job interview, I finally knew in my gut what I wanted to do: turn down the job and invest in myself, going full-time for a year to see if I could make it work.

What surprised me most about people's reactions was how some of my closest friends were encouraging me not to do that. Many said, "Well, can't you just do both—take the job and do Greatest Story on the side?" It upset me initially. I first thought, *Do you think I'll fail? Why don't you believe in me?*

Then something became very clear to me: Their advice was actually about what they would tell themselves to do. They were freaked out (as I was, to some degree) about the financial and emotional risks it would take to run a business full-time. They were all in careers or in school at the time. To my friends, those were risks *they* wouldn't take, so they advised me accordingly.

I'm really glad this happened because it taught me an important lesson: Sometimes people you love, and who love you, will discourage you. They'll discourage you from taking big risks, living with passion, and making changes. Often, it all comes down to a simple, understandable explanation: They'd be afraid to be in your shoes. They wouldn't want to get hurt, and they certainly don't want you to.

I love my friends. I value their perspectives immensely. But as I experienced at this pivotal crossroads of my life, sometimes someone's perspective is going to come from a powerful place of their own fears and insecurities. These friends loved me and didn't want to see me suffer, get hurt, or fail.

The worries they shared with me all came from a very personal and caring place. I always knew that. But ultimately, their concerns weren't giving me the energy I needed to do what I knew deep down I had to do. This is why I listened to their voices but didn't defer to them. I took my own risk (alongside my own fear and insecurities) and jumped in.

Going full-time is one of the best life decisions I've ever made. I took big, scary emotional and financial risks by doing this, and they've paid off in spades in the years that have followed. This decision has taught me to take more risks and embrace more change, possibly even more so than leaving Hollywood did.

And you should know that I'm still so appreciative of those friends who originally discouraged me from taking that big leap. They've fully supported every step I've taken from that first major decision onward. They've helped me stuff envelopes, come to my business workshops, shared my posts, and encouraged me when I've struggled and failed along the way (in-between the successes and the high points of entrepreneurship).

As much as I was surprised and disappointed when some of those dearest to me voiced their caution, the pushback was valuable for me. It showed me how to handle disapproval and discouragement better, and how to put advice in perspective and context. It also made me realize that with a choice like this, somebody had to go first.

By nature, most of us are scared to take big steps and leaps into the future. We are conditioned to take the safe route—to take the stable job while you grow the side hustle, for example. Someone had to be first and shake things up, and this particular time it was me.

I like to think that this jump I made into the unknown (and all that's happened since) has inspired my friends. I wonder if it's showed them that it's okay to break the mold and leap—even when not everybody's buying in. I know that this story has helped others to realize they can do the same, even if their friends or their family don't quite get it.

If your friends and family have surprised you with how they're handling your ideas or actions on what to do next, I encourage you to listen and to think about where their concerns may really be coming from. The people who love you have your best interests at heart, but they can't always see what's possible for you or even for themselves. Sometimes, you have to show *them*. Sometimes, you need to be the one to surprise them.

On your way to reinvention, you may even need to surprise yourself. That also happened for me. It took many crossroads in my career to realize that when I was thinking of changing my life and career, I was always looking for permission from others instead of myself.

Permission to chase my dreams. Permission to change my game plan. Permission to quit. Permission to reinvent myself.

I was so concerned with how everyone would react for a very long time. After years passed and I finally did take big steps and told people that I was taking action, I was surprised by how everyone reacted. But most of all, I surprised myself.

When I finally made the big life decisions for myself, and put to rest the need for buy-in and approval from everyone in my life, I made it possible to be my own agent of change. Rather than looking to others, I have had to tell myself *my own permission was enough.* And when I did that, I transformed my life beyond anything I could have imagined.

Sometimes we have to make deals with ourselves to give ourselves permission, like when I had to say, "Okay, I'll give myself a year" to turn down that ad agency job. I needed to make the deal with myself to make it possible, but that didn't come from anyone but me. I had full control over it and I still do.

For you to be able to give yourself permission to try to put to rest the worries of what others will say and do, you must be ready to acknowledge the very real permission you need to give yourself first: permission to fail.

CHAPTER 10

"But what if I fail?"

PERMISSION:

YOU HAVE PERMISSION TO FAIL

Failures Will Help You Grow

We named the dog Indiana Jones. Given this, I'm not sure what we expected to happen. I should've seen the next part coming.

It was fall 2016. My husband, Gus, and I had been going through a rough season in our lives. We'd been trying to have children for more than a year at that point, and Christmas was coming. I was starting to think that we were ready for a new challenge: getting a dog. I had so much love to give, but the baby thing wasn't happening, so I thought maybe a dog would be a way to invest that part of myself. In my head, that dog was definitely Dug from the movie *Up*, a big, lovable golden retriever. We couldn't get a golden retriever because Gus is allergic, so instead, we started thinking about a goldendoodle. I'd heard they make great family dogs and, from what I understood from basic research, they shared a lot in common with golden retrievers, as they are part golden and part poodle.

I was nervous committing to this, though. I definitely didn't want to be that person who got a dog to compensate for the fact that she couldn't have a baby, or the person who got a puppy as a Christmas gift and then felt like she had to re-home him or her within the year because it didn't work out. However, I did want to practice the thing that I had been learning for so many years, and what I've been talking to you about in this book. I do believe that you have to do the things that scare you and that you can't get out of your mind. That's what I was doing by deciding to get a goldendoodle puppy for Christmas: jumping in, feeling the fear, and doing it anyway!

Indiana Jones "Indy" Franceschi was born on March 9, 2017. We brought her home on May 6, 2017. She was so little she could fit inside my Indiana Jones fedora from our wedding reception. We

One deceptively cute puppy.
(Photos by Gus Franceschi and the author)

were so excited for this adventure with her and to bring her home into our lives.

I remember hearing her bark for the very first time. *What a novelty!* Little did I know that bark would be forever ingrained in my memory. During that first weekend, I got the first sense that *Uh oh . . . this is not going to be easy.* I was on solo puppy duty; Gus had exams to study for. It's not that I thought it was going to be easy. It's that I thought that Indy and I would share a connection. I thought that we would create a special bond that would transcend all of the hard work of raising a puppy and a dog.

However, what I started to realize was that Indy had a boundless energy. As you've been learning about me in this book, I'm what you might call an "inside kid." I don't run unless someone is chasing me. I'm the girl who always finished last in P.E. class when we ran the mile. And Indy was quite the opposite. She had amazing levels of energy! She was unstoppable. Apparently, I hadn't learned this before we got her, but goldendoodles can be this way. They can be incredibly smart with "a mind of their own," and insatiable for playtime and attention. I missed that—somehow I missed that. On my best days of chasing her and walking her and doing everything I could to spend time with her, I would get her back in the house and then she'd just look at me, at attention, like *"Okay, what now?"*

No matter what I did, I started to feel that I could never make her happy. I began to feel like Indy was a bomb that had gone off in my life. She was pulling at me during everything I needed to do, all the time. And during the time that I spent with her, she didn't seem very interested in me or spending time with me. Each time that happened, when I felt Indy didn't really care if I was there or not and

I couldn't keep up with her energy, I felt like a failure. And that was the last thing I needed in that season of life, as I faced infertility and feeling like a failure on a recurring 30-day basis.

My biggest fear came to pass: I realized that Indy and I were not going to work out. And it broke my heart. I wanted to love Indy more than anything in the world. But Gus and I were at the end of our ropes, and we knew, deep down, the uncomfortable truth was that Indy wasn't a good fit for us and maybe I wasn't cut out to have a dog at all (at least not at that time).

I felt so selfish and stupid. It didn't help that some people went on to tell me, "Oh yeah I was a little worried about you getting such a big dog" or "Yeah, you guys were crazy to get that dog!" Oy, that hurt. It's not like I hadn't done any research; I just clearly didn't do enough on her breed. Also, I had no way to know up-front that Indy was going to be this boundless ball of energy who would make me feel the way I felt. You can't know a dog's exact personality just from his or her breed, and I'd never had a dog before. I'd never even had a real, non-fish pet before! While others saw my mistake coming, for my own sake, I know that I had to ask the question in order to find out the answer. Warts and all, that's exactly what I had done.

Dealing with the reality of Indy was new and hard and, frankly, deeply embarrassing. I started texting some of my friends, beginning with the very ones who I was worried would judge me because they had rescued dogs and gone through hell with puppies. I wanted their permission and their approval, but I was sort of terrified that they would think I was an idiot.

But here's what they told me: stories. They told me about friends whose dogs had to be adopted by their parents because they just couldn't handle them, or that their lives or jobs changed unexpectedly. They also told me that it was okay—that having a pet isn't for everybody and that raising a puppy isn't for everybody. They shared that I wouldn't be selfish to give Indy up. In fact, I would have been selfish to keep her, if I wasn't truly able to love on her and to give her the happy life that she deserved. And I wasn't. *Indy was a great dog. She just wasn't a great dog for me.*

As it turned out, she was a great dog for my cousin Hannah. She and her boyfriend (now fiancé), Alex, volunteered to take care of Indy, and we made plans for that transition. Our last day with Indy was Sunday, August 6, 2017, exactly three months to the day that we had brought her home. And after having so much trouble with her—countless visits to the vet, me screaming in the house because there'd been a mess to come home to—we got the perfect day with her. We took her on a walk, snuggled with her on the couch, and then delivered her just 15 minutes from our house to Hannah and Alex in nearby Chapel Hill.

I held her, gave her a kiss on her forehead, and told her, "Thank you, Indy, for being the dog you are, and I'm glad you're now my cousin."

We drove off. I cried a little bit, but Gus and I instantly felt tremendous relief. I felt the mantle of responsibility, inferiority, and insecurity fall off of my shoulders. I knew I didn't have to be what Indy needed me to be anymore. I could now close the three-month chapter that was probably the most stressful period of my entire life.

I failed with Indy. I owned that then, and I own it now. I've said that to many people since I realized it myself. And my friends and my family sometimes correct me and say, *"No, Annie. It's okay. You didn't fail: You learned."* They're right. I did learn. But I failed. I took a significant risk, I did what I'm telling you to do in this book, and nevertheless I failed hardcore—big and messy, throwing myself on the floor in tears kind of failure. And I wasn't sure how to feel about that at the time.

A few months later, I went to see Indy for the first time since giving her up. My cousin Ashley and I headed over to Hannah and Alex's for dinner. As we approached the door, I was nervous to see Indy. I remember thinking, *Will she even remember me? I'm pretty sure she could care less about me, but we'll see.*

When I walked in, Indy made a beeline for me! She jumped on me. She was so excited to see me! And I was so relieved. She was truly happy with Hannah and Alex. There she was: my puppy cousin, who sweetly remembered all the tricks that Gus and I had taught her at puppy school.

I made my peace with Indy in that moment. I was finally able to put the hardness of this story behind me. At the time, I could also see that, through my failure, came Hannah and Alex's happiness. Hannah is a runner, a personal trainer, and the owner of H & Arrow Fitness and Pure Barre Asheville in Asheville, North Carolina. And in many ways, she's just like Indy. They are both fiercely independent, sweet, and wonderful ladies who are excited to go and do things. She and Indy are the perfect match for each other.

Because I was willing to admit my mistakes—because I was willing to say that I failed—Hannah and Alex get to have a family with Indy. Indy gets to grow up with owners who adore her. Though they playfully call her "the white terror," they love her with and for her idiosyncrasies.

The happy family.
(Photo by Charles Consky)

The awesome thing is that now I, too, can feel free to love Indy. I don't have to resent her. I can admit that I made a mistake and also see that mistake doesn't have to end in sadness. I needed to close this chapter and move on. But even still, in many ways, I needed to open the door in the first place.

Since I failed even though I practiced the advice within this book in getting Indy, will I turn to you and say, "Don't do the things that scare you because you might fail?" Quite the opposite.

I will tell you that you have to do these things. You have to open the door and walk through it. You have to take the next step forward,

Reunited as cousins.
(Photo by Hannah Fleishman)

because you do not know what will happen. You may succeed tremendously, as I have been able to do with so many risks I've taken. But you may also fall flat on your face.

You may fail in ways you could never imagine. But failures will help you grow. They will help you know what it is you need, and what you don't. You have to try anyway. That is what having permission to fail is all about: knowing that in order to try something, failure may happen along the way.

I failed, and yet great, life-changing things happened because of it. I learned so much. I embrace the fact that I have made mistakes and that I do have regrets, but those things can co-exist alongside happiness. We cannot always win the day, and the reality is we won't. We cannot always make the best decision or the right decision. But what we can do is make *a* decision.

This is your permission to fail.

TAKE ACTION EXERCISE

UNCOVER THE GOOD AND GROWTH IN YOUR FAILURES

HAVE HANDY: Pen and paper or a computer

1. I want you to do something that sounds painful. Think back and brainstorm all of the significant mistakes and failures you've had in your whole life—as many as you can think of. *(No, this is not meant to be torture of any sort. I promise there's a point.)*
2. Create a two-column table on paper or in Excel/Google Sheets.
3. Label the left column "Notable Failures" and make a list of your "ugly" things there.
4. Label the column on the right "Good Things that Happened Anyway."
5. Now, challenge yourself to think of and list at least one or two good things that happened wholly because or partially because of those awful things.

Here are a few of my own as an example:

NOTABLE FAILURES	GOOD THINGS THAT HAPPENED ANYWAY
Indy turned out to be a terrible fit for our family, and I endured the most stressful three months of my life and one of my most biggest personal failures.	• My cousin Hannah and her fiancé, Alex, got their dream dog, whom they adore, and seeing them happy makes me happy. • I learned a lot about what I want and don't want in a dog and in any sort of dependent situation (pet, baby, what have you). This 'ish is hard work and I'm glad I know more about what to expect now!
At Disney, I got put on movie titles that didn't have a lot of budget or priority, and it led to me almost getting fired! (For the full story, see Chapter 8.)	• This gave me an opportunity to be brutally honest with my boss, and led to the team reinventing my job and giving me the best incarnation of my film industry career there'd ever be.

NOTABLE FAILURES	GOOD THINGS THAT HAPPENED ANYWAY
In 2010, I bombed a series of eight interviews with 16 people that I had for becoming a production assistant on feature animated films. After an unexpected production shut down, it was my shot to keep from getting laid off from a role at Disney Animation (my first position at the company).	• If I'd gotten that job, I would have gone down a much different path, and likely been let go and had to switch jobs multiple times over the past few years (because that's the nature of working in production). • In the interview process, I learned what a bad fit I was for the people I would have worked closely with. If I'd gotten the job, I would have been tempted to take it, but I don't think I would have been happy. • I would have definitely missed the opportunity to join and becoming a founding member of the Franchise Management team at the studio. That job came up about six weeks after this one fizzled.
I was a finalist for the Morehead Scholarship to UNC–Chapel Hill, a really prestigious program that covers four years of tuition. I didn't care much about getting it until the finalist weekend, when I learned how cool it was and how much they allow the students to do creative things as Morehead Scholars. Once I cared about getting it, of course, I wasn't selected at the very last step. Crushing defeat.	• I was *this* close to going to UNC–Chapel Hill for this scholarship but when I didn't get it, I knew in my gut I was meant to go to Duke. Leaving out the rivalry for a second, going to Duke transformed my life and my vision for my career. And I made the most of the university's resources, getting them to invest tens of thousands of dollars into my idea for an annual filmmaking competition. I'm not sure I would have been thinking that way if I hadn't been exposed to the Morehead program, and I'm so grateful that ultimately Duke was where I went for school. *(Side note: Go Devils!)*

NOTABLE FAILURES	GOOD THINGS THAT HAPPENED ANYWAY
A total #fail, I got flustered at a screening and accidentally didn't recognize Bob Iger, *aka the CEO of Disney (!)*. I was an idiot and asked him if he'd move a seat over. He sort of stared me as I realized my mistake and another employee grabbed my arm to pull me away.	• I didn't die of embarrassment, so that's good. • One of my friends at the company told me later that week that it was a good thing. She said that he likes being treated like a normal person. She might have been saying it spare my feelings, but it worked in either case. • It makes a great story to tell at dinner parties.

Whatever's on your list of failures, I hope you find that going through and admitting the good things that came after gives you some encouragement. More than anything, I hope it gives you the solace of knowing you have permission to fail.

There's Good
in Unfixable Things

I can still remember my life when there was nothing in my universe that was "unfixable," no event in my life that I'd never be able to make right. There was nothing that had happened to me at that point that couldn't be overcome or improved or changed with enough work, a positive attitude, and/or luck. Then when I was 17, one day, without warning, my mom passed away.

It was my first unfixable milestone. In an instant, my mom was gone and there it was: something in my life that was unmovable, unchangeable, forever hard—forever in place. Maybe you've had something like this happen to you. Perhaps something has happened as a result of your own failings.

The thing to remember and embrace is that life is full of unfixable things. We burn bridges despite our best intentions; we lose jobs (I have—twice); we break up with friends and significant others or they break our hearts. Our lives themselves are the very definition of unfixable. In being alive, it's inevitable that we will one day die, at a point that will be forever fixed in time for us and for those who love us.

Some say, "Everything happens for a reason." I used to believe that, but I'm not sure if I do anymore. After being diagnosed with terminal cancer, author Kate Bowler wrote her memoir, *Everything Happens for a Reason: And Other Lies I've Loved.* She points out in the book that this very sentiment oddly and unfairly implies that we are fated for bad things to happen, and that perhaps we deserve them.

Instead, *I think that while everything doesn't happen "for a reason," there can be good that comes from everything that happens.*

I will always miss my mother. I will always wish that I had had more time with her and that she'd had more life to live. But misery and grief were not the only things her death gave me. Her passing has made me stronger. It led me to be a better daughter, a better friend, and a better business owner. It made me aware and grateful for her legacy and mindful of making my own. It reminded me of how short and precious life can be, and that my voice matters.

If you give yourself permission to fail and then you do—if you make a mistake that is big and unfixable—you need to know that there is life afterward. Though things don't always happen for a reason, there is still good ahead in your life after unfixable things. You can't let the possibility of something unfixable happening keep you from answering the important questions of your life.

Ask the Question
to Know the Answer

Whatever it is you want to do next, you can ponder and think about all the scenarios that could happen. You can live in a cycle of fear and doubt for as long as you choose. But taking action is the only real way to ask the question and learn its answer.

Consider some of the questions (and their answers) I've been sharing with you from my own story so far:

> *What will happen if I get a puppy?*
> *What will happen if I start a blog and online shop on the side?*
> *What will happen if I'm honest with my boss about how I feel?*
> *What will happen if I quit a job I love without a plan?*
> *What will happen if I go full-time in my business?*

On just these questions, I have spent an impressive number of hours, weeks, months, and years wondering and worrying about all the things that might happen if I were to actually answer them through action. I can tell you with absolute certainty that it's been far better to have asked these questions, and learned their answers, than to continue living in fear and wondering what the answers might be.

You know the millions of theories, thoughts, and worries you have about what's coming next in your life? The big questions that keep you up at night? Nearly all of them will never, ever happen. For every question you have, only *one* real thing is going to happen to you around the corner if you choose to ask it. Only one thing will come to pass, not the hundreds of possibilities that stop you in your tracks. And the only way to know 100% for sure what that thing will be is simply to ask the question—to ask the universe: *By trying, what will happen?*

Ask the question by:

> *Doing the thing.*
> *Risking the failure.*
> *Putting yourself out there.*
> *Creating change.*

As every bump in the road I've shared with you in this book has shown, there is no way out but through. While I am sure your story and your circumstances are different from mine, it's nonetheless true that you can't avoid the "diet and exercise" and the reality of asking big questions of yourself. The only way to get your own answer is to ask your own question: *Hey universe? What will happen if I do this? If I reinvent myself? If I take this risk?*

Will you ask it?

CHAPTER 11

DOUBT:

*"But how will I ever get to a life
and career that I love?"*

PERMISSION:

GIVE YOURSELF PERMISSION TO TRY

Do What Both Scares and Captivates You

I have found that, throughout my life and career, two things are always true of the little ideas that keep me up at night—the stuff that raises its hand in the back of my brain:

1. *They freak me out.*
2. *They fascinate me.*

They repeat, over and over, a chorus in my soul—until I finally listen, until I say them out loud, and until I act on them. One of these things has been professional speaking.

In 2015, I had done some speaking at school growing up, but nothing formal—just honor club speeches and that sort of thing. At Disney, my job was to write and create presentations that would be given by high-level executives about upcoming movies. Through that experience and on into my life as an entrepreneur, I had it on my heart to become a professional speaker.

But, of course, I was terrified to try it. The closest I'd come was recording a 10-minute presentation as a voice-over for author Richie Norton (I shared that story in Chapter 4). Throughout my career, I'd always been the girl who built the content, not the person who gave the talk. The content often wasn't even mine; it was Mickey's. So I sat on this idea for years. I let it sit in the back of my head, fascinating me. I thought about it for months. I spoke to a photographer named Dana who had posted about looking for a speaker for her Wilmington Weddings group. We talked and I shared that I was interested, but I didn't hear anything more, and more months passed by.

Though I was nervous to try it, the thought was still nagging at me. I decided to get it out of my head through an accountability trick. I talked about this desire to speak with my small group of fellow women entrepreneurs at a monthly meetup. *"Hey, I'm thinking about becoming a speaker but I'm pretty scared to go after it."*

What followed were a ton of encouragement, ideas, and cheers from my friends. Suddenly, this little nagging thought was a real thing, and I was getting good feedback on it. *Maybe I should give myself permission to give this a go?* I went home from the meeting and emailed Dana to say hi and ask if she was still interested in speakers. She wrote right back. She was looking for a speaker the next month and asked me!

I nervously prepared my first presentation with hours of work spent designing slides, scripting, and telling my story of taking risks and living your strengths. I wasn't sure if it was any good, but I pushed myself forward. My friend Ashlee drove with me to Wilmington for the speaking engagement in front of 30 wedding entrepreneurs. I was really nervous to get up and start talking, but when I did, it was as if my heart just pressed "Play." It came as natural to me as anything ever has in my entire life. I was elated and invigorated. I felt born to do this: to use my voice and my content to help other people own their story.

The event was a hit. It would kick off the past three years of my career as a professional speaker. Since that evening, I've given more than 70 presentations, become a paid speaker, and spoken to thousands of people across the Southeast on branding and entrepreneurship. And it all happened because I gave myself the permission to talk about it and, then, the permission to try it. It was that thing I couldn't get out of my head, and there was clearly a reason why.

Through this and other adventures in my life, what I have come to realize is that this magical combination that happens to me—this mixture of fear and fascination—happens when I'm considering taking a powerful risk in my life.

I've long loved the poem "The Road Not Taken" by Robert Frost. You know, the one about two roads diverging in the woods, and taking the one less traveled by?

My version might go like this:

> *"One road kept me up at night, calling and calling.*
> *I thought of a million reasons not to walk down it—*
> *all the bad things that could happen on the journey."*

The thing is that I'd spend days, weeks, months, and sometimes years planning how to take that first step and go down that road at some point—at some time. But life, as it continues to show me, whether I fail or succeed, is about jumping in with both feet!

It's giving yourself the "okay":

> *. . . that your first plans didn't work out,*
> *. . . to make space to create a life you love,*
> *. . . to embrace the freedom to reinvent yourself,*
> *. . . to summon the courage to take risks,*
> *. . . to fail,*
> *. . . and to try.*

Originally, when I was planning this book, I was thinking it was going to feature a permission slip where I could literally give you permission to do the things: big and small, what both scares and captivates you, what keeps you up at night.

And then I realized two things:

1. Legally, do I want to be giving people permission? I mean, what if you never went to medical school and you're taking this as permission to go for it and DIY some surgery!?

2. You don't need my permission. Or anyone else's.

All you need is your own permission.

Permission to try.
Permission to fail.
Permission to do, and to ask, and to learn, and even to feel lost.

If you do nothing else, I invite you to do just that. Whatever it is that is on your mind—the thing you constantly consider but feel afraid (for any and every reason) to do—stop sitting on it. Go do it.

Give yourself what you have always deserved:
permission to try.

This Is Your Permission Slip

In this final Take Action Exercise, you have my permission to tear the following page right out of the book and fill it out for yourself. Whatever it is, big or small, that's on your heart right now: give yourself permission to try it.

Find more permission slips at permissiontotry.com.

PERMISSION SLIP

I, —————————————————————,

give myself **permission to try**

—————————————————————.

From the book *Permission to Try* by Annie Franceschi | Get more permission slips at permissiontotry.com.

You Know How
to Continue This Story

I have a presentation that I give to small business owners on the five steps you can take to put your best foot forward with your branding. It's a really comprehensive overview of best practices in 90 minutes. Every time I present it, I imagine that by the end, the audience may feel a bit overwhelmed, behind, or even discouraged with how they have been marketing and branding themselves.

That's why I always close the talk with something meant to lift everybody back up and keep them moving forward. I tell them, *You've already taken the first step.* By being at the seminar, these entrepreneurs are already taking important action to grow their businesses.

I say the same thing to you: *You've already taken the first step.*

The good news is that it's no longer about the first step. You've already taken the first step by picking up this book (I'll even give you credit if you just skimmed to this page, in fact). You took an action—a step forward in a new direction—by picking up this book and considering what might be possible in your life.

What to do next is pretty simple and a whole less intimidating than taking a first step. Just take a second one.

You already know what step 2 is, so go do it.

JUST FOR YOU

———

Re-Read This as You Need To

I learned a huge lesson during the year it's taken me to write this book: the cycle of needing to give yourself permission and remembering how to do that is definitely going to repeat itself.

You may use this book to get unstuck, give yourself permission, and take the big risks you need to take. And that may lead to incredible things in your life. I truly hope it does. But even as I've shared in the stories here, the cycle will repeat itself. You'll leap and then, months or years later, you'll find yourself struggling and wondering about changing your life or career again.

I know that as I was writing this and dealing with new challenges in my life and in my business, I found myself wishing that this darn book was done so I could go back through it, dog-ear the pages, and underline the advice. So in many ways, this book is a love letter to both my past and my future selves. And if at the end of the day, nobody else buys this book but my dad and my husband, there'll be a copy around to encourage me, and that will be more than enough.

But if this book has helped you, I hope you keep it handy on your shelf. I hope that you wear the pages down, scribble your notes in the margins, and come back to it when you feel weary. I hope that you will buy copies for friends who need it and lend your well-loved copy to someone you love.

I hope that now and in the future, this book will be here for you when you need that shot of courage. *Let it be a reminder that you don't need anyone to save you. You have been your own hero all along.*

A Handy-Dandy Time Line

In order to present this book as the pep talk it's intended to be, I deliberately told some stories out of order. For reference, enjoy this quick at-a-glance of key dates and events across my story, from childhood to now.

MAY 26, 1985 — I am born! Parents are thrilled, and *Muppet Babies* is in its second season.

SUMMER 2008 — I move from NC to LA and begin working at Lionsgate.

Chapter 2

SUMMER 2009 — I leave Lionsgate for a gig at Disney (first at Disney Animation, then in March 2010 at the Studios).

NOVEMBER 2012 — I start writing my anniemade blog as part of opening an online shop to sell "bouquet pins."

Chapter 3

FEBRUARY 2013 — A bride named Bridget finds me via Google.

Chapter 3

MARCH 2013 — I get uncomfortably close to being fired and my job changes overnight.

Chapter 8

APRIL 2013 — We make our decision to leave LA over bugers at In-N-Out.

Chapter 5

JULY 2013 — I get up the courage to tell people and give notice at work.

Chapter 9

SEPTEMBER 4, 2013 — My last day at Disney. We move to NC a week later.

Chapter 7

OCTOBER 25, 2013 — I officially register Greatest Story Creative as an LLC in NC, but continue looking for jobs.

JANUARY 25, 2014 — I decide to go full-time with Greatest Story.

Chapters 8 and 9

SEPTEMBER 2014 — Richie Norton gives me a chance to create a presentation for his course.

Chapter 4

MARCH 2015 — I have my first real speaking gig in Wilmington, NC.

Chapter 11

AUGUST 2016 — We're diagnosed with infertility.

Chapters 2 and 7

MAY–AUGUST 2017 — We get a puppy, then we un-get the puppy.

Chapter 10

SEPTEMBER 26, 2017 — Gus gets into Elon!

Chapter 4

OCTOBER 25, 2018 — Greatest Story Creative turns five and I fulfill my bucket list dream of writing a book.

Every chapter

And the adventure continues . . .

Resources for You

I was dreaming about all the goodies I wanted to put in the back of the book for you, like my other favorite book recommendations for finding your new purpose, taking risks, starting businesses etc., free templates, activities, and more. But then I thought that I'd love to keep that stuff current and have a way to connect with you.

I also realized that we have an awesome thing known as the internet. So rather than print resources that can go out of date, and that I can't add to, in a book, I'm putting everything together for you online and updating it as I continue trying things myself.

DISCOVER THE *PERMISSION TO TRY* ONLINE RESOURCE LIBRARY

You're invited to enjoy the *Permission to Try* online resource library! At the website below, you can sign up for access to free templates, a PDF of exercises, updates on future books, and more great content.

www.permissiontotry.com

To access the readers-only area of the resource library, please note you'll need this access code:
takethe2ndstep

(This is our secret password, now that we're friends!)

You may also enjoy some of the titles I referenced in the book itself, many of which I read during this season of reinvention:

- *Steal Like an Artist,* Austin Kleon
- *Cultivate,* Lara Casey
- *Make it Happen,* Lara Casey
- *The Power of Starting Something Stupid,* Richie Norton
- *Quitter,* Jon Acuff
- *The Total Money Makeover,* Dave Ramsey
- *Financial Peace,* Dave Ramsey
- *Everything Happens for a Reason: And Other Lies I've Loved,* Kate Bowler

And if you're curious to read them, as of this writing, my old anniemade blog posts are live on anniefranceschi.com/anniemade.

Share Your
Permission to Try Story

You've heard my story. Now I want to hear yours! What have you tried or what are you going to try, now that this book is in your hands?

Share your story with me and the Permission to Try community by emailing it to:

permission@anniefranceschi.com

Questions?
Here's How to Reach Me

I'm here for you and excited for what second step
you're about to take!

Say hi and reach me directly at
annie@anniefranceschi.com.

Behind the Scenes

This book got its start from a ton of Post-its and a writing retreat in Wrightsville Beach, North Carolina in August 2017.

If you're wondering if you have a book in you, I highly recommend putting everything you know and like to talk about onto Post-its and going from there.

A crazy three days of writing work at the beach. Had writers block, went way off my agenda, floated in an inflatable donut. But I'm leaving with an outline for my first book. Crazy!

As you have seen or will soon see by doing the Take Action Exercises in this book, let it be known that much can come from making lists and actually putting pen to paper.

(All photos by the author)

Acknowledgments

Gus, Dad, and Minda—I get to live a life that I love every day thanks to you. Thank you for always believing in me and for picking me up during all of those real-life moments when I'm about a million miles from Annie with the gold star on her head.

Mom—I loved having this opportunity to share your story because there are so many people who need to hear it. When I get to heaven, I'm sure of two things: 1) You'll have notes, and 2) You'll have told everyone all about this book because you're so proud of me.

My incredible friends and family—Thank you for being a part of my story these 30-some years and for your tremendous encouragement to write a book in the first place. Throughout this process, I've felt like you've always envisioned me writing one, like it was inevitable. When I've doubted myself and felt like giving up along the way, it's been your support, Facebook likes, text messages, panda memes, and hugs that have kept me writing. *And a very special shoutout to everyone who rocked being on the book's launch team!*

My amazing clients—Because of you, I get to love what I do for a career. Thank you for entrusting me to do the most rewarding work in the world: giving you ways to see your own value, to start businesses you care about, and to tell your stories.

My beta readers: Jacqueline Collins, Annie Flaherty, Christina Hubbard, Holly Landis, Avalon Levey, Ashley Noga, Blair Overman, Dana Publicover, James Ranson, and Faith—I was terrified to send you the manuscript, but I'll be forever glad I did and so will everyone who reads this book. Thank you for helping make *Permission to Try* what it is.

Jodi Brandon—I'm so grateful for your belief in my book, for your stellar developmental and copyediting skills, and for being the first to confirm as a publishing professional that this book was strong and that it was not, in fact, as I'd feared: garbage.

Faith Teasley—Hey Boo. Without you, I'd still be using a carefully cropped photograph from my wedding as a headshot. Thank you for the majority of the gorgeous photography in this book, all the ways you make my life better between your friendship and talent, and the opportunity to work as your intern on photo shoot days. I'd like a letter of recommendation for future employers, please.

Brett and Jessica Donar—Not only were you our super-chill wedding photographers, you also helped me launch my anniemade blog and ultimately Greatest Story. I can't thank you enough for your willingness to let me use photos from our wedding to promote my work in those early years. It was game-changing for me, and I'm so happy to have the opportunity to feature a few of your photographs in the book.

Sarah Potts—My fabulous virtual assistant and real-life friend. Thank you for being the very first to "hear" this book when I'd send you audio files to transcribe. It's like you were in on the demo tapes, and I couldn't have gotten a lot of this down on paper without your swift and excellent help.

Diana Needham—I so value your enthusiastic support of me, my business, and this book. Your wisdom in how to launch and market *Permission to Try* has been invaluable and your friendship has been even better.

The Hornaday Family—You have one pretty sweet beach house in Wrightsville, NC. Thank you for letting me cover your beautiful walls in giant Post-its as I dreamed up and began to outline this book in August 2017 during my work retreat with Chrissy and Harper.

Austin Kleon—Thank you for writing *Steal Like an Artist*. Not only did it give me permission to reinvent myself, it also showed me that it was possible to write this book.

Lara Casey—So grateful to you for the Making Things Happen conference in March 2013, for everyone I've met who's changed my life as a result, for the wisdom to name my fears, and for your caring friendship.

Richie Norton—Because your book changed my life and especially because you gave me the opportunity to put my money where my mouth was by creating a presentation for you.

Bridget Bogee—I'm forever glad Google connected us. Thank you for seeing the value in me that I couldn't yet see. For two people who've yet to meet in person, you've had a profound effect on my life, this book, and my perspective on people that I'll always appreciate.

Dana Laymon—I'm so grateful that you invited me to speak to your networking group in March 2015 even though it was my first real gig ever. Thanks for taking a chance on me. It launched a part of my career that I deeply enjoy.

Adele Michal—Your teaching, guidance, and friendship have fundamentally changed my life and the trajectory of my career and business. I'm so excited to tell everyone the story of how you helped

About the Author

Annie Franceschi believes that your life is your greatest story. She is an author, professional speaker, and the brand creator behind Greatest Story Creative®, a small business branding agency. A Duke University graduate with more than 10 years working in storytelling, Annie built her career in franchise management of major movies at The Walt Disney Studios in California. In 2013, Annie quit her dream job at Disney to become an entrepreneur. Now, having branded more than 70 businesses, advised hundreds, and spoken for thousands, Annie is a passionate creative partner to small business owners who need the name, logo, words, and website that show their value, tell their story, and grow their business. She lives in Durham, NC, with her favorite person and husband, Gus.

Connect with Annie online:

- *Personal Website:* anniefranceschi.com
- *For Speaking Inquiries:* anniefranceschi.com/speaking
- *Business Website:* greateststorycreative.com
- *LinkedIn:* linkedin.com/in/anniefranceschi
- *Instagram:* instagram.com/annie.franceschi

CPSIA information can be obtained
at www.ICGtesting.com
Printed in the USA
LVHW04s1954031018
592296LV00005B/16/P

me save my business from the brink of collapse and fall back in love with it at the same time, but that'll have to wait until Book 2.

My work family from Disney and everyone who made leaving the film industry and Los Angeles one of the toughest choices of my life—Thank you for believing in me, skipping out to lunch at Burbank Town Center, and giving me a chance to show you what I could do. I miss you. Come visit!

My incredible teachers at Fayetteville Academy and Duke University—Thanks especially to Ellen Olson Brooks, Lulie Harry, and the late Otis and Barbara Lambert for giving me the knowledge, space, respect, and support to explore my talents and abilities during the awkwardness of high school. And thank you, Elisabeth Benfey, for the countless opportunities you gave me to create amazing things for you, for Duke, and for your family. Oh, and "Magna Carta 1215," Mrs. Harry.

Kermit, Piggy, Fozzie, Animal, Bunsen, Beaker, and the rest of the Muppets—Thanks for being my friends since childhood, helping me rediscover what I've always loved, and for the "sincere love of silliness" you always inspire me to have.

And finally, Indy—Thanks for keeping me humble and for the learning opportunity. I hear you are still one crazy B. Be nice to your parents.